MOVEMENT-BASED LEARNING:
Academic Concepts and Physical Activity for Ages Three through Eight

Rhonda L. Clements, Ed.D.
Physical Education and Sport Pedagogy
Manhattanville College
Purchase, New York

Sharon L. Schneider, M.S.
Department of Curriculum and Teaching
Hofstra University
Hempstead, New York

National Association for Sport and Physical Education
an association of the American Alliance for Health, Physical Education, Recreation and Dance

Address order to: AAHPERD Publications, P.O. Box 385, Oxon Hill, MD 20750-0385, call 1-800-321-0789, or order online at www.naspeinfo.org.
Order Stock No. 304-10300

Printed in Canada
ISBN#: 0-88314-916-8
Suggested citation for this book:

Clements, R. L., & Schneider, S. L. (2006). *Movement-based learning: Academic concepts and physical activity for ages three through eight.* Reston, VA: National Association for Sport and Physical Education.

CONTENTS

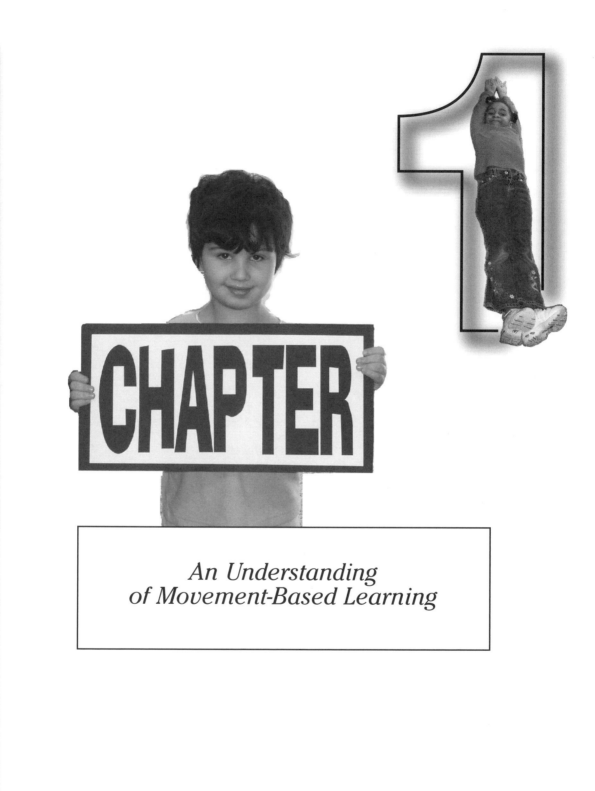

CHAPTER

An Understanding
of Movement-Based Learning

"We are only limited by our imagination."
~
The Authors

An Understanding of Movement-Based Learning

INTRODUCTION

This book is intended for all who touch the lives of children within childcare settings and the lower grades in elementary schools, whether that be physical educators, classroom teachers, or daycare specialists who are searching for innovative "use-it-today" ideas for teaching young children. Teacher trainers in physical education will find original movement content presented in an easy-to-use format, and teacher trainers in early childhood and elementary school education will discover two innovative approaches to teaching many core skills and concepts mandated in their curriculum. Individuals working within an inclusive setting or in a self-contained classroom can easily adapt the activities to meet the requirements found in Individualized Education Programs (IEP) and 504 Accommodation Plans. Recess or lunchtime specialists, after-school specialists, and parents who homeschool their children will also find the contents of this book dynamic and appropriate because of the noncompetitive nature of the activities. Members of parent-teacher organizations will be delighted that the majority of the learning experiences do not require equipment, or a specialized setting. Finally, it is our hope that curriculum specialists and school administrators will find novel concepts and activities to enhance their existing programs. Our goal is to provide original and innovative content that will increase the child's understanding through movement-based learning.

OVERVIEW

Each chapter in this book focuses on academic concepts that are age- and stage-appropriate for the child and progress from simple to more complex physical challenges. Chapter One gives the reader a brief foundation of movement-based learning by identifying the key components of the imitative and movement exploration approach to teaching basic movement skills and concepts. Key characteristics and practical examples of the two approaches are discussed, and implementation strategies are provided. The creative use of props will also be explored in this chapter.

In Chapter Two, children build upon their existing movement vocabulary and linguistics while discovering the joy of specialized movement activities and movement narratives. In Chapter Three, the activities are aimed at increasing the child's understanding of healthful living. All activities focus on increasing the child's understanding of the body, and the importance of eating healthy foods. Chapter Four is designed to foster community awareness, as children identify the integral members who are part of their home community, and the roles these people play within their everyday activities. Chapter Five helps the child develop basic environmental awareness while acquiring an appreciation for living creatures. Chapter Six explores assessment tools and techniques available to assist the teacher in evaluating a student's level of success utilizing a movement-based approach to learning. Resources are also provided for further investigative reading.

Each movement-based learning experience is presented in a simplified lesson plan for the beginning or novice teacher. This format identifies: (a) NASPE's National Standard for Physical Education that is being emphasized, (b) the primary learning objective, (c) any recommended materials or equipment, (d) individual or partner learning experiences, (e) a whole-group learning experience, and (f) creative closure questions.

RATIONALE FOR MOVEMENT-BASED LEARNING

From birth, children have a natural desire to explore and experience new challenges. For the youngest child, learning occurs through play as parents introduce their child to the immediate environment. As children reach the age of three, their yearning to explore and experience new things still exists; however, parents and other adults are charged with the task of increasing the child's understanding beyond what is introduced in the home setting. This includes teaching basic concepts reflecting the child's body, vocabulary, community setting, and expanded environment. The ongoing question is how to best convey these new concepts and understandings without interrupting the child's need and desire for physical activity. This book is based on the belief that children can acquire many of the concepts common to the academic program and be able to demonstrate nationally recognized physical outcomes through movement-based learning. In addition, preschool through age eight children should acquire an even greater love for learning because they are physically engaged in the learning process.

THE NEED FOR DAILY PHYSICAL ACTIVITY

The National Association for Sport and Physical Education (NASPE) published *Active Start: A Statement of Physical Activity Guidelines for Children: Birth to Five Years* in 2002. This document was instrumental in providing teachers who work with young children a clearer understanding of the importance of daily physical activity. The following identifies the five suggested guidelines for preschool children:

Guideline 1. Preschoolers should accumulate at least 60 minutes daily of structured physical activity.

Guideline 2. Preschoolers should engage in at least 60 minutes and up to several hours of daily, unstructured physical activity and should not be sedentary for more than 60 minutes at a time except when sleeping.

Guideline 3. Preschoolers should develop competence in movement skills that are building blocks for more complex movement tasks.

Guideline 4. Preschoolers should have indoor and outdoor areas that meet or exceed recommended safety standards for performing large muscle activities.

Guideline 5. Individuals responsible for the well-being of preschoolers should be aware of the importance of physical activity and facilitate the child's movement skills.

The authors of this book recognize that 60 minutes per day of suggested "structured" movement content requires careful planning on the part of the teacher. Implementation considerations include identifying movement experiences that are age- and stage-appropriate and selecting an appropriate method(s) to teach the content. Many teachers will also confront issues concerning limited space and equipment. Some school administrators and daycare directors may also have difficulty finding qualified individuals who can facilitate the child's movement skills (as recommended in Guideline Five), and assess the lesson's objectives and outcomes. This book strives to address these typical concerns.

PHYSICAL ACTIVITY GUIDELINES FOR CHILDREN IN GRADES K-2

The National Association for Sport and Physical Education also recognized the need for written suggestions concerning the importance of physical activity for children in elementary school. Therefore, the second edition of *Physical Activity for Children: A Statement of Guidelines for Children Ages 5-12* (NASPE, 2004b) became available. This document is instrumental in using research findings to make the case for daily physical activity. The following identifies the suggested guidelines for children in kindergarten through grade two. The authors highly suggest that all readers secure a copy of the complete document (see NASPE Resources at the end of this book) to obtain a more in-depth interpretation of each guideline, as well as a valuable listing of definitions, concepts, and ways to encourage increased physical activity in their school setting.

Guideline 1: Children should accumulate at least 60 minutes, and up to several hours, of age-appropriate physical activity on all, or most days of the week. The daily accumulation should include moderate and vigorous physical activity, with the majority of the time being spent in activity that is intermittent in nature.

Guideline 2: Children should participate in several bouts of physical activity lasting 15 minutes or more each day.

Guideline 3: Children should participate each day in a variety of age-appropriate physical activities designed to achieve optimal health, wellness, fitness, and performance benefits.

Guideline 4: Extended periods (periods of two hours or more) of inactivity are discouraged for children, especially during the daytime hours.

NATIONAL STANDARDS FOR PHYSICAL EDUCATION (K-2)

To further assist the teacher, NASPE published its second edition of *Moving into the Future: National Standards for Physical Education* (2004a). These national learning standards were developed for children in kindergarten through grade 12. The following cites the learning standards that pertain to children ages five through eight.

Standard 1: Demonstrates competency in motor skills and movement patterns needed to perform a variety of physical activities

Standard 2: Demonstrates understanding of movement concepts, principles, strategies, and tactics as they apply to the learning and performance of physical activities

Standard 3: Participates regularly in physical activity

Standard 4: Achieves and maintains a health-enhancing level of physical fitness

Standard 5: Exhibits responsible personal and social behavior that respects self and others in physical activity settings

Standard 6: Values physical activity for health, enjoyment, challenge, self-expression, and/or social interaction

AN UNDERSTANDING OF MOVEMENT-BASED LEARNING

Movement-based learning requires teachers to select age- and stage-appropriate activities for children. This of course means matching the content with the child's physical, social, and cognitive development—a task easier said than done. To assist in this process, the authors created and used the following five criteria to assess the extent that each learning experience would coincide with the child's level of development:

First, all learning experiences should be based on a foundation of age-appropriate movement skills. The level of difficulty was field-tested in a variety of settings to determine if all children found success, and yet were adequately challenged. *Second,* all activities for this age level should encourage the child to use his or her imagination and provide opportunities for expressive movement, since this age level delights in knowing that they can use their bodies to show how they are feeling. *Third,* the learning experiences should foster cooperative versus competitive behavior. *Fourth,* the learning experiences should encourage full participation from the class. This does not mean that all children in a small group situation need to be physically active all the time. It does imply that children are not waiting in line to participate, or being eliminated while they are participating in a whole-group learning experience. *Finally,* all learning experiences should be reflective of curriculum content common to preschool through grade two.

MOVEMENT-BASED SKILLS: Moderate to Vigorous Physical Activity
I can move throughout the playing area by...

ADVANCING: To move forward or ahead. *The little girl advanced to the front of the line.*

CHARGING: To rush at with force. *The elephants charged through the jungle, stomping on trees and scaring other animals.*

CLIMBING: To move upward using both the hands and the feet. *The little boy climbed to the top of the tree to sit inside his tree house.*

CRAWLING: To move slowly with arms, hands, knees, belly, and legs along the floor. *The baby crawled on the floor to get his bottle.*

CREEPING: To move slowly on hands and knees close to the ground. *The little mouse crept along the floor looking for cheese.*

DARTING: To move suddenly and swiftly in short quick movements. *The frog darted its tongue to catch the fly.*

DASHING: To move with sudden speed. *When the sudden rainstorm came, the little girl dashed to get out of the rain.*

EXPLORING: To travel throughout an unfamiliar space for purposes of discovery. *People rode in a submarine and explored the ocean floor.*

FLYING: To move through the air with wings. *The birds flew south for the winter.*

GALLOPING: A gliding step, moving forward by keeping one foot in front. *The cowboy held on very tightly as his horse galloped to the corral.*

HIDING: To get out of sight. *The children hid under the bed.*

HOPPING: To jump using one foot. *The children hopped on one foot while playing hopscotch.*

JUMPING: To take off with both feet, and land on two feet. *The kangaroo jumped through the bushes.*

LEAPING: To propel into the air while stretching one leg forward and landing on that foot. *Ballerinas leaped in the air.*

MARCHING: To walk with regular, long, even steps. *The firefighters marched in the parade.*

POUNCING: To seize down upon. *The lion pounced upon his prey.*

ROLLING: To turn over and over. *The ball rolled down the hill.*

RUNNING: To move faster than a walk. *The elephant was scared of the mouse, and ran away as quickly as he could.*

RUSHING: To move or act quickly. *The children rushed to the movie, so they wouldn't be late.*

SCAMPERING: Using small steps to move quickly. *The squirrel scampered about, gathering nuts for the winter.*

SCATTERING: To separate and go in many directions. *After raking the leaves, a strong wind blew and scattered the leaves over the yard.*

SCUFFLING: To scrape or drag the feet. *The children scuffled their bare feet in the sand.*

SCURRYING: To move lightly and quickly. *The mouse scurried to his hole.*

SEARCHING: To look for an object, person, or thing. *The boy searched in his pockets and found his lucky penny.*

SHUFFLING: To walk using small steps and keeping the feet and knees together. *While walking home, the boy shuffled his feet and buried his hands in his pockets.*

SKATING: To glide along ice. *The children skated on the frozen pond.*

SLIDING: To move one foot over a surface to the side and quickly move the other foot to it. *The girl danced and slid one foot to meet the other.*

SLITHERING: To move along by gliding. *The snake slithered under the rock.*

SNEAKING: To move in a sly or secret way. *The children sneaked an extra cookie from the cooling cookie pan.*

SOARING: To rise, fly, or glide high in the air. *The birds soared high in the sky near the top of the mountain.*

STROLLING: To walk in a slow, relaxed way. *The family strolled along the boardwalk to watch the sunset.*

STRUTTING: To walk in a swaggering or proud manner. *The peacock strutted to show off his colorful feathers.*

SURROUNDING: To be on all sides, encircled. *The fence surrounded a schoolyard.*

SWIMMING: To move through water using the whole body. *The children were swimming in the pool with their friends.*

TIP-TOEING: To walk softly on the fronts of the toes. *The little girl tiptoed out of the room so not to wake up her grandfather.*

TRAMPING: To walk with a heavy step. *Mom had hot chocolate ready for us when we tramped into the house with snow-covered boots.*

TRUDGING: To walk slowly, or with effort. *The children were so tired from their long walk that they trudged the last few blocks home.*

WADDLING: To sway from side to side using short steps. *Penguins and ducks waddled as they walked in the zoo.*

WALKING: To move on feet at a steady pace. *The men walked each day to exercise and stay healthy.*

WANDERING: To move without a destination or purpose. *Children wandered about looking for brightly colored leaves.*

MOVEMENT-BASED SKILLS: Moderate Physical Activity
I can stay in one place and use my body parts to...

ARCH: To form a curved structure. *The cat arched his back.*

BALANCE: To be in a steady, stable position. *The clown lost his balance but did not fall.*

BEND: To become curved or crooked. *The boy bent down to tie his sneaker.*

BOB: Quick up and down movement. *The fishing pole float bobbed up and down in the water.*

BOUNCE: To come back or up after hitting the surface. *The children bounced up and down on the trampoline.*

BURST: To break open suddenly and violently. *It was so noisy when the fireworks display burst in the sky.*

CLAP: To strike hands together noisily and quickly. *The people showed their appreciation when they clapped their hands as loud and as long as they could.*

COLLAPSE: To fall down suddenly or cave in. *The little girl collapsed on her bed and went right to sleep.*

CRUMBLE: To break or fall into small pieces. *The cookie crumbled into cookie crumbs.*

CRUNCH: To grind or crush loudly. *The broken eggshells crunched under his boots.*

CURL: To move in a round shape. *She tucked in her chin, curled her body and did a perfect forward roll.*

DANGLE: To hang loosely. *The lady's long earrings dangled from her ears.*

DEFLATE: To collapse by letting air out. *The car tire deflated after rolling over a nail.*

DODGE: To avoid by moving quickly from side to side. *The rabbit dodged away from the fox.*

DUCK: To lower the head or body quickly. *The boy ducked his head so he would not hit the low tree branch.*

EXPAND: To make large. *When we inhaled deeply, our lungs expanded.*

FLUTTER: To flap the wings quickly, but not move. *The fly's wings fluttered when it was stuck in the spider's web.*

FREEZE: To become motionless or fixed. *The children froze their bodies in funny shapes when the music stopped.*

GRAB: To seize suddenly, snatch. *The boy grabbed his jacket and ran to catch the bus.*

HANG: To be attached by the upper end only. To fasten something from above only, without support from below. *The man hung the picture up on the wall.*

HOLD: To keep in the arms or hands. *She held her shiny new penny very tightly in her hand.*

HOVER: To stay in one place in the air. *The helicopter hovered over the helipad.*

INFLATE: To expand by filling with air. *He huffed, puffed, and inflated all the beach balls.*

JERK: To move with sudden, sharp movements. *The pony jerked the reins from her hands.*

KNEEL: To get down on bent knees. *The girl knelt down to play with the puppy.*

LEAN: To slant from an upward position, while supporting one's weight. *He leaned down to do a push-up.*

LIE DOWN: To be in a flat, resting position. *We laid down on the bed to sleep.*

LIFT: To raise upward. *The girl lifted her trophy for all to see.*

MELT: To lessen or fade away gradually, dissolve. *The butter melted in the frying pan.*

PRESS: To put steady force against. *The boy pressed the elevator button to go to the fifth floor.*

PULL: To tug towards oneself. *The children pulled at the rope.*

PUSH: To press away from oneself. *The snowplow pushed the snow.*

REACH: To stretch out or extend. *He reached his arm out to help his friend stand up.*

RISE: To get up from lying, sitting, or kneeling. *When we woke up, we rose from our bed.*

SHAKE: To move with short, quick movements. *The dog shook off the water from his fur.*

SHIVER: To shake out of control. *The children shivered because they were so cold from playing in the snow.*

SHRINK: To decrease in size. *The hamburger was cooked too long and shrank to look like a piece of charcoal.*

SHUDDER: To tremble or shiver suddenly. *We shuddered when we watched a scary movie.*

SINK: To move to a low level. *This rock sank to the bottom of the pool.*

SPIN: To rotate at a high speed. *The ride spun us around and we became dizzy.*

SQUEEZE: To press together with force. *We squeezed juice from an orange.*

STAMP: To put the foot down heavily and noisily. *Dinosaurs stamped their big feet and made the earth shake.*

STAND: To stay in an upright position. *The boy stood by the tree.*

STRETCH: To become a greater length or width. *The people stretched their muscles to make them longer.*

SWAY: To move back and forth. *The trees swayed in the strong wind.*

SWING: To move back and forth, turn on a hinge. *The monkeys swung on vines from tree to tree.*

TOPPLE: To fall over. *The house of cards toppled over.*

TREMBLE: To shake from fear or cold. *The kitten trembled from the cold rain.*

TUG: To pull strongly. *The tugboat is pulling the barge.*

TURN: To move around a center, rotate. *The child turned the doorknob.*

VIBRATE: To move back and forth quickly. *The airplane flew so low to the home that all the walls vibrated.*

WHIRL: To spin quickly. *The children held hands and whirled around to the music.*

WIGGLE: To move parts or the whole body in a swaying motion. *The pig wiggled his tail.*

WOBBLE: To move from side to side in a shaky manner. *The car wobbled as it went down the street on its four flat tires.*

THE IMITATIVE APPROACH

Movement-based learning also utilizes two similar teaching approaches to spark the children's interest in learning new skills. The first approach is the imitative approach to learning. The word "imitative" has a Latin origin *(imitari)* meaning, "to make a copy of" and "likeness." The English adopted the term at the end of the 16th century and used it to describe a behavior or quality to emulate that all children and adults possess. This belief stems from the basic premise that mankind and womankind are imitative creatures with similar interests, forms of communication, and ways of moving. We all engage in an endless change of behavior patterns that make us eat alike, dress alike, act alike, and play and move in similar ways. Concerning the young child, Froebel (1826/1887) said, "What the child imitates, he begins to understand." Effective teachers utilize the young child's urge to imitate his or her parents' and siblings' verbal and physical behaviors. These teachers become models for the child's further development.

The importance of providing a model for the child to imitate has long been recognized as one way children acquire identity and language, through imitating words overheard (Bandura, 1977; Erickson, 1963; Piaget, 1962; Singer, 1973; Skinner, 1974). The value of imitation is also apparent in many abstract forms of communication, including dance or rhythms, music, and movement. For example, dance professionals use an imitative approach when they prompt the child to follow the words and movements of an action poem or song. They are also using the imitative approach whenever children are asked to repeat simple rhythmical beats using handheld instruments such as a drum, tambourine, lummi sticks, or when they are prompted to duplicate the slapping, clapping, and pounding actions common to hand-clapping chants. In addition, music provides opportunities to imitate different types of sounds and moods as selected by the teacher.

Physical educators, early childhood specialists, and classroom teachers can find great success when using the imitative approach to introduce basic movement skills and concepts appropriate to the child's level of readiness. For example, the preschool child's movement vocabulary is greatly expanded each time the teacher conveys the proper name of a physical skill such as galloping, and then demonstrates the movements for the child to copy. A typical teacher delivery might ask the child, "Make-believe you are a herd of wild horses and follow me as we gallop forward."

In the simplest sense, teachers can challenge the preschool child to mimic such quotations as "still as a photograph," "busy as a bee," "light as a feather," "cold as ice," "stiff as a board," or "sly as a fox." The children can also use their bodies to duplicate a wide variety of feelings and expressions such as acting fearless, frightened, angry, and gloomy. Other examples include demonstrating action words and assuming the body gestures and facial expressions of storybook characters in a movement narrative, which are included throughout this book.

The teacher's behavior can also encourage the preschool child to mimic novel ways of moving such as duplicating the common movements of animals, or to follow the teacher's movements along imaginary pathways, or to reproduce a combination of movements after observing the teacher's performance. In each learning experience, the teacher displays enthusiasm and great facial expression to spark the child's continued involvement.

Teachers who favor the imitative approach in movement-based learning recognize the importance of fostering the young child's imagination. They realize that many preschool children become easily frustrated and develop anxiety that inhibits further participation unless a model is available to duplicate or copy. This is especially true if a child has no

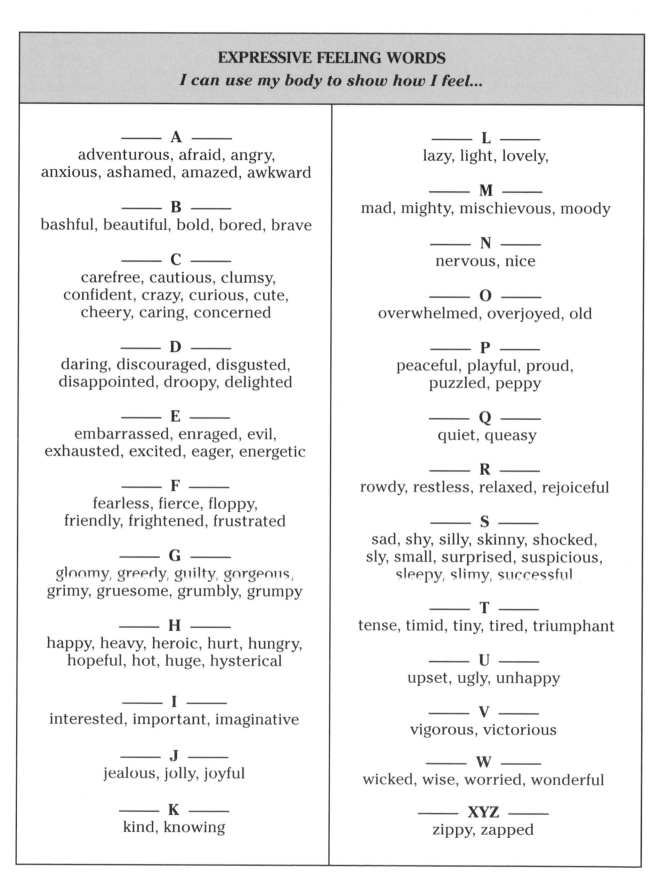

EXPRESSIVE FEELING WORDS
I can use my body to show how I feel...

—— **A** ——
adventurous, afraid, angry,
anxious, ashamed, amazed, awkward

—— **B** ——
bashful, beautiful, bold, bored, brave

—— **C** ——
carefree, cautious, clumsy,
confident, crazy, curious, cute,
cheery, caring, concerned

—— **D** ——
daring, discouraged, disgusted,
disappointed, droopy, delighted

—— **E** ——
embarrassed, enraged, evil,
exhausted, excited, eager, energetic

—— **F** ——
fearless, fierce, floppy,
friendly, frightened, frustrated

—— **G** ——
gloomy, greedy, guilty, gorgeous,
grimy, gruesome, grumbly, grumpy

—— **H** ——
happy, heavy, heroic, hurt, hungry,
hopeful, hot, huge, hysterical

—— **I** ——
interested, important, imaginative

—— **J** ——
jealous, jolly, joyful

—— **K** ——
kind, knowing

—— **L** ——
lazy, light, lovely,

—— **M** ——
mad, mighty, mischievous, moody

—— **N** ——
nervous, nice

—— **O** ——
overwhelmed, overjoyed, old

—— **P** ——
peaceful, playful, proud,
puzzled, peppy

—— **Q** ——
quiet, queasy

—— **R** ——
rowdy, restless, relaxed, rejoiceful

—— **S** ——
sad, shy, silly, skinny, shocked,
sly, small, surprised, suspicious,
sleepy, slimy, successful

—— **T** ——
tense, timid, tiny, tired, triumphant

—— **U** ——
upset, ugly, unhappy

—— **V** ——
vigorous, victorious

—— **W** ——
wicked, wise, worried, wonderful

—— **XYZ** ——
zippy, zapped

concept of how to perform a physical task. When working with three- and four-year- old children, the teacher uses carefully selected cues that are appropriate to the child's stage of development. Among others, these typical teacher deliveries might include, "Imagine...," "What if...," "Make-believe...," "Create...," "Build a...," and "Pretend you are...," to prompt the child's movement response.

Imagine your foot is a pencil and you are drawing a picture on the floor.

What if your hand was a paint brush? Make some long and squiggly marks.

Make-believe you are a kangaroo jumping along a path.

Create the shape of an orange with your body.

Build a tunnel with your legs.

Pretend you are a soap bubble floating high in the sky until you pop!

The challenge is to select content that has meaning or is relevant to the child. For example, if the child has no conception or mental image of how to "pretend to be a spaceship blasting," or "make-believe you are paddling a canoe," some discussion or desired action must take place. Furthermore, asking a child to "pretend to be a football player," or "make- believe that you are a basketball player," will only have meaning to the child if he or she has truly been exposed to that character's movements.

TEACHER'S WORDING

Make-believe...   *Pretend...*   *Create...*   *Make up...*   *Suppose...*
Imagine you are...   *Act as if...*   *Move like...*   *Copy me...*
Follow me...   *Build...*   *My turn... now your turn...*

IMITATION

Child copies or follows, repeats, mirrors, echoes, or shadows

---

Teachers who favor the imitative approach with preschool children are inclined to believe that imitative experiences do not stifle the child's ability for creativity and self-expression, since all humans need a foundation from which to pull creative thoughts, ideas, and knowledge. Imitation serves as a foundation on which higher order thinking skills can be constructed. They also see the importance of planning tasks that are within the child's range of challenge, and they capitalize on the child's interests. Another aspect of this approach is that the young child is not hampered by his or her lack of vocabulary and inability to follow verbal directions, since the greatest emphasis is on the use of sight.

Our teacher training programs must not fail to recognize that the two-year-old child only has a vocabulary of approximately 200 words. Between the ages of three and four, a child will more than quadruple his or her vocabulary from about 1,000 to well over 4,000 words, acquiring new words at the astonishing rate of about 9 words per day. However, it isn't until the child is at least six years of age with a vocabulary of approximately 8,000 to 14,000 words that he or she can truly be expected to comprehend the complex directions that teachers typically use. Therefore, the use of the imitative approach for preschool children can serve as a means for learning since three-year-old children can only carry out the sequence of one simple direction, and four-year-old children are able to hold only two ideas or directions in the mind (e.g., "Terry, please pick up the ball, and put it into the storage bin."). It also provides a foundation for greater movement challenges taught through movement exploration.

MOVEMENT EXPLORATION

Assuming that most children have acquired a variety of new movement concepts and movement skills through the use of the imitative approach, it is now time for the teacher to capitalize on the children's past experiences that form the structure into which they can assimilate new learning. Children ages five through eight can greatly benefit from the teacher's use of movement exploration approach as a means of learning additional movement skills and more classroom concepts. From a theoretical standpoint, the teacher plays a critical role in expanding the child's awareness of and ability to perform movement skills, even though they do not serve as a model for the child to imitate, since ultimately older children must perform the cognitive operations to construct meaning.

The role of the teacher is to ask a series of planned movement questions that challenge the child to explore a variety of movement possibilities. For example, if the primary objective is to increase the child's awareness of different types of shapes and specific shapes the body can make, the teacher can ask questions containing objects or things that are common to the child's cognitive awareness. These could include asking the child, "Who can show me a round apple shape with their body?" Or, "Is it possible to make a twisted pretzel shape using your body?" Children at this age level are also able to make comparisons between their body parts and those of other living creatures. For example, "Crickets hear with their legs. Can you point to the body parts that we use to hear sound?" When exploring different speeds, by which the body can move, questions can be based on images of speed boats, jet airplanes, and race cars as well as the movements of snails and turtles. When teaching the child where the body can move through space, the questions can focus on moving at a high level where birds fly, or a low level where ants crawl. In most instances, the teacher can use descriptive words within each question to encourage the child to rely on previously learned knowledge and experiences.

The desire to have children physically respond in a variety of creative ways and situations is greater than the need to have children obtain advanced skills for movement efficiency. For example, the skill of jumping can be used to express a feeling (e.g., "Show me who can jump up and down with excitement."); as a form of association (e.g., "Who can use all of their muscles to jump like a frog?"); as a manner of moving over or around objects (e.g., "Can you jump over the box, now around the box?"); as a method of becoming physically fit ("Let's see if our hearts beat faster when we continue to jump up and down."); and as a manner of socialization ("Is it possible to jump up at a high level and high five your partner's hand?"). In these sample movement exploration questions and phrases, the need to execute the jump at maximum efficiency is not as important as the need for the child to obtain a greater understanding of how the jump can be used in different situations and in creative ways.

Therefore, the teacher uses movement exploration as a means for the child to use the skills acquired in preschool, and elaborates on those skills by organizing and processing

*Can you...?   Determine the best way to...   Discover different ways...
Explore other ways...   Find another way to...
How many different body parts...?   How would you...?   How do you...?
How can you...?   How else would you...?   How many ways...?
Is it possible...?   In how many ways...?   Invent a new way...
See how many different ways...   See if you can...   Show how...
Show me a different way to...   Who can...?   What does a...?
What ways can you...?   What kinds of things...?   Try changing...
Try to find another...   Try it again, another way...*

the information in the form of multiple movement responses. This approach also insures active participation, provides opportunities for creative thinking with classmates, increases the child's responsibility in following directions, and fosters the child's self-esteem with feelings reflecting "I can do it!"

In order to more clearly understand the difference between the types of methodologies that are considered age- and stage-appropriate for preschool versus children in kindergarten through grade two, it may be helpful to consider the earlier example involving the imitative approach in which a preschool class was asked to, "Make-believe you are a herd of wild horses, and follow me as we gallop forward." This challenge offered a model for the child to duplicate when learning how to gallop. When teaching five- to eight-year-old children, the task can be expanded by using movement exploration questions in the following sample action rhyme:

How Horses Move
The teacher presents the following:
"We can use our bodies and learn how different kinds of horses move." "Can you begin by making the sound of horses hooves by slapping your legs with your hands?" "Now, let's see who can move to the actions of different horses."

Wild mustangs run free,
Galloping across the open prairie.
Can you gallop and keep one foot in front of your body?

Bucking broncos jump and kick,
As if jumping on a pogo stick.
Show me how you can jump up and down like a bucking bronco.

Beautiful show horses stand tall as they prance.
It sometimes looks like a fancy dance.
How would you prance around our play area like a proud show horse?

Tiny, prancing Shetland Ponies are small.
Giant, plodding work horses are tall.
See if you can prance while being small. Now, to be tall, stretch upward like the work horse.

Cowboys and cowgirls ride horses to chase cows.
Work horses are used on farms to pull heavy plows.
Is it possible to move like a cowboy or cowgirl riding on a horse?

Thoroughbred horses are used in a horse race.
They gallop around a circle at a fast pace.
How quickly can you gallop in a circle like a race horse?

Merry-go-round horses move up and down,
As the carousel goes round and round.
Who can raise and lower their body while moving in a circle like the merry-go-round horse?

Real horses stomp their feet and paw the ground,
Then leap and jump, bucking all around.
Who can leap forward? Now jump and buck by stretching your body.

Horses also walk, run, trot, and jump.
Then shake all over, from their head to their rump.
Determine the best way to walk, run, and trot like a horse.

This original learning experience makes use of the older child's previously learned movement skills and classroom concepts. It also uses movement exploration to challenge the child's creative thinking for greater movement-based learning.

MOVEMENT-BASED CONCEPTS

Overall, the contents of this book were created to satisfy several purposes. As stated earlier, the authors realize that many educators do not have ample equipment or spacious gymnasiums when conducting movement-based learning experiences. For this reason, the majority of this book's activities can be successfully performed in a limited space, or in a classroom setting without expensive equipment. The more critical objective for each learning experience is aimed at increasing the child's understanding of movement. This understanding encompasses the following concepts:

INCREASED BODY AWARENESS

Face: Forehead, ears, mouth, hair, lips, eyelashes, chin, jaw, nose, eyebrows, tongue, cheeks, teeth, eyes, dimples

Upper: Hands, fingers, palms, wrists, forearms, chest, back, elbows, neck, shoulders, stomach, head

Lower: Feet, toes, heels, ankles, calves, knees, legs, hips, thighs

---

INCREASED SPATIAL AWARENESS

Personal Space: Awareness of the area within the child's reach, where no other child's body is occupying space

General Space: Awareness of the area encompassing the entire play area

Direction: The line along which the body moves
(forward, backward, sideways, upward, downward)

Range: Awareness of the distance of objects in relation to the body
(near/far, long/short, above/below, narrow/wide)

Level: Awareness of horizontal planes (low, medium, high)

Pathway: Awareness of the route the body moves through space
(straight, twisted, curved, circular, zigzag)

INCREASED UNDERSTANDING OF HOW THE BODY MOVES

Speed: Awareness of how fast the body or parts of the body can move
(how quickly or how slowly)

Force: Awareness of force needed to perform a task
(heavy, light, strong, weak, hard, soft, harsh, gentle)

Flow: Awareness of and the ability to link movements together smoothly

---

INCREASED RELATIONSHIPS WITH PEERS OR OBJECTS

Moving with a Classmate: The ability to copy, meet, lead, follow, or pass

Placing the Body: Above, below, over, under, near, far, in front of, behind, to the side, around, between, into, in back of, alongside, next to, down, underneath, up above, on top of, inside, outside, next to, through

Comparisons: Bigger than, smaller than, slower than, faster than, greater than, less than, shorter than, taller than

COMMON MOVEMENT SKILLS AND CHALLENGES

Walking

Teaching Cues for Walking:

1. Stand tall with your chin level with the floor.
2. Walk and gently swing your arms at the side of the body. Don't over swing.
3. Your head should be kept up, and your eyes should be focused ahead.
4. Your stride should be natural, while trying to avoid any unnecessary up-down motion.
5. Hold your stomach in while you walk.
6. Your heel is the first part of your foot to touch the ground.

Imitative:

- Imagine you are walking in a parade, along a twisted path in the woods, in gooey mud, on slippery ice, on eggs, stepping over boxes, on the moon.
- Pretend you are walking up a hill, now a steep mountain.
- Let's walk on our heels, toes, side of the foot.
- Pretend to be a metal robot and walk throughout our playing area.
- Slowly lower your body while walking, and then raise yourself up again.
- Follow me and walk with a smooth gliding step.
- Pretend to be a giant with very large legs.
- Walk in different shapes—circles, square, triangle, the shape of the number eight.
- Act as if you are feeling very proud while walking and swinging your arms at your sides.
- Suppose you were walking on hot sand.

Movement Exploration:

- How many tiny or giant steps does it take you to cross this playing area?
- Can you walk and change your direction? Level? Speed?
- Who can express joy when walking? Sorrow? Anger? A different feeling?
- Is it possible to walk on only your toes? Heels? Inside of foot? Outside?
- Discover how many ways you can walk.
- Show me how you can walk and change direction after every eight steps.
- Try walking around the room pushing your head toward the ceiling.
- Find a way to walk like an elephant, bear, giraffe, deer, and cat.
- Show me how you can walk and make different shapes—circle, triangle, square, diamond.
- How would heavy winds affect the way a person walks? Show me.

Running

Teaching Cues for Running:

1. Keep your head up while running and your eyes forward, so that you do not bump into other children.
2. Push off with the front part of your foot.
3. Bend your arms and swing them close to the sides of your body.
4. Lift your knees while you run.
5. If you want to run fast, your knees must be bent and lifted more.

Imitative:

- Let's run in place and lift our knees high.
- Run lightly upon your toes throughout the playing area. Be careful not to bump other children.
- Pretend you are a car moving very quickly, and run in a round racetrack shape.
- Suppose you pick an imaginary spot away from you. Run to it and return without bumping into anyone.
- Make-believe you are a wild horse and slap your knees as you run.
- Follow me as I run using different steps (e.g., tiny, long, light, heavy, crisscross, wide).
- Move like a ghost and run with your arms waving in the air.
- Create the letter "O" as you run. Now form the letters "M," "Z," "B," "C," and "D."
- Make-believe that you are running in a deep forest and dashing from side to side to avoid the low branches.
- Act as if you are very excited and happy while running.

Movement Exploration:

- Who can run in the greatest number of different ways?
- Can you combine a run with any other kind of movement?
- Show me how you can run using your arms in a way other than by swinging them forward and backward.
- Is it possible to run very close to the floor and change on a signal to go to your highest running position?
- Try running side-by-side with a partner and staying at the same speed.
- Who can run in rhythm in a group of three? In a group of four?
- See if you can run fast and stop suddenly on my signal.
- Can you run to (a specific point in the playing area) and return to your original position?
- Determine the best way to take as few running steps as possible to get to a spot.
- Discover the best way to run at a medium speed (i.e., jogging), now at a top speed (i.e., sprinting).

Jumping
Teaching Cues for Jumping:

1. Lean in and bend your knees and ankles before taking off for a jump.
2. Swing your arms back and then forward as fast as you can. Jump so your heels clear the floor.
3. Land with your knees bent.
4. Land lightly on your toes, balls, and heels—not flat footed.

Imitative:

- Imagine you are a kernel of corn being heated. Show me how you would jump as you become a piece of popcorn.
- What if you could write letters on the floor by jumping? Create the letter "O" as you jump. Now create the letters "X," "L," "N," "P," and "S."
- Make-believe you are a kangaroo, and jump forward as far as possible.
- Follow me as I jump and create a large number "eight."
- Pretend you are jumping over small rocks.
- Create different ways you can jump over a puddle of water without getting wet.
- Pretend you are a playground ball, and see how many different heights you can bounce.

- Move like a frog jumping from one lily pad to the next one. Remember to land on all fours.
- Follow me as we jump in the shape of a circle, square, triangle.
- My turn to jump high and reach up to touch the sky. Now it's your turn.

Movement Exploration:
- Can you move a different body part at the height of your jump?
- How many jumps would it take you to move from where you are standing to that spot in the playing area?
- Who can find a way to jump up high while moving your body forward?
- Is it possible to jump and cross your legs while in the air?
- Find ways to clap your hands while jumping in the air.
- Discover new ways to jump over the line on the floor.
- Show me how you jump up and down like a basketball being dribbled on the basketball court.
- See if you can look like a diver who is jumping up and down on the diving board.
- What are some ways you can jump and use your body to keep (imaginary) balloons floating in the air. Don't let any of them touch the floor.
- Invent one way to jump with a partner, and then give your partner a high five.

Hopping
Teaching Cues for Hopping:
1. Keep your head and chest upright.
2. Use your arms for balance when you hop.
3. Hop on one foot.
4. Bend your knee as you land lightly on your toes, balls, and heel.
5. If you want to increase the height of the hop, you must swing your arms upward.

Imitative:
- Imagine you are a grasshopper. Take three giant hops and land next to a pretty flower.
- What if your feet could draw on the floor? Can you create the first letter in your name while hopping?
- Create a circle, square, triangle while hopping.
- Pretend we are barefoot and walking on hot sand. Hop on one foot and then the other, saying, "Ouch!! Ooooch!! Hot, hot, hot."
- Suppose you just finished swimming and have water in your ears. Show me how you would hop on one foot and shake your head to get that water out.
- Hop in the shape of the letter "O." Now create the following letters by hopping: "U," "J," "A," "T," and "G."
- Copy me as I hop forward, backward, sideward, and in a zigzag line.
- Follow me as we hop on one foot and then the other.
- My turn to hop and land lightly with my knee bent. Now your turn.
- Pretend to be an airplane while you hop with your arms extended out to the sides.

Movement Exploration:
- Can you change levels of your upper body while hopping?
- How many different hopping animals or insects can you create with your body?
- Who can hop from one foot to another? Now, can you clap hands each time one foot lands on the floor?

- Is it possible to hop higher and higher each time you try? Try this five times to see how high off the ground you can hop.
- Show me how fast you can hop. Now hop slowly.
- Invent ways to hop with your body in different positions.
- Try to hop and land as lightly as you can on one foot.
- Discover how far you can hop, how high you can hop.
- Can you hold your free foot while hopping?
- What ways can you hop in rhythm with a partner, three classmates, four, five, the entire class?

Galloping

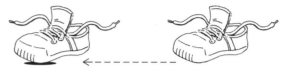

Teaching Cues for Galloping:
1. Keep your head and chest upright.
2. Keep one foot in front of your body.
3. Step forward with one foot and bring the other foot to it.
4. Move forward with the same leg always in front.
5. Let your arms relax and allow them to swing forward and back freely.

Imitative:
- Imagine you are a pony trying to gallop for the very first time. How would you perform your first gallop?
- What if one partner leads and the other partner follows while you gallop throughout the playing space.
- Make-believe you are galloping while riding a pony. Hold your hands out so you can grip the reins tightly.
- Pretend you are a pony galloping around the room.
- Suppose you are a horse and are trying to gallop with two riders on your back.
- Act as if you are a tired horse galloping back to the stable for the night.
- Move like a wild stallion, moving at a fast gallop and then stopping for a drink of water.
- Copy me as I gallop in the shape of letter "Z."
- Follow me as we change our lead foot after three gallops, five, ten.
- My turn to gallop, stop, and change direction. Now your turn.

Movement Exploration:
- Can you gallop in rhythm with a partner? Now find another set of partners to create a small herd of ponies. Can you gallop in rhythm with the other ponies in your herd?
- Invent a new way to gallop with a partner.
- Who can gallop in the shape of a circle, triangle, square, on a diagonal?
- Is it possible to gallop and change direction whenever I say, "Change?" Are you ready? Let's start. Change.
- Show me how you can make large galloping movements, small galloping movements.
- Can you gallop in the shape of the letters "S," "P," "Z," "L," and "C?"
- Try galloping as fast as you can, slow, hard, soft.
- Discover how other body parts can move while you gallop.
- Can you change the size of your gallops?
- Who can gallop like a race horse approaching the finish line?

Slide Step
Teaching Cues for Sliding:

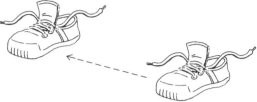

1. Move one foot to the side and quickly move the other foot to it.
2. Slide your feet along the floor.
3. Lead with the same foot.
4. Remember that your body is moving sideways.
5. Try not to bounce.

Imitative:
- Imagine you are a dancer who slides to music. Listen to the rhythm of the music and slide.
- Make-believe your feet are paint brushes as you slide along the floor.
- Create an ice skating pond by sliding along the ice on your skates.
- Pretend you are a paint brush and brush a figure eight onto the floor as you slide.
- Act as if you are looking into a mirror. With a partner, one is the leader and the other follows the leader's movements while sliding. Then switch roles.
- Move as if you were sliding with glue on the bottom of both sneakers.
- Copy me as we slide in the shape of a circle, square, triangle.
- Follow me as we slide to one side of the room and then back again.
- What if you were sliding and clapping at the same time.
- I will take three sliding steps in this direction. Now your turn.

Movement Exploration:
- Can you slide face to face, then back to back with a partner?
- How many different body parts can you move while you slide?
- Who can combine a slide with another type of movement?
- Is it possible to make long sliding movements, shorter ones? Now try other lengths.
- Find a way to slide as a group in a circle. In what other patterns can your group slide in?
- Can you find a way to slide in a circle shape?
- Try changing speeds as you slide.
- Discover ways to slide while changing your body level.
- Try to move like a basketball player sliding across the basketball court.
- Show me how you can slide with a partner while holding hands.

Skipping—For Children Ages Five and Older
Teaching Cues for Skipping:
1. Keep your head and chest upright.
2. Lift your knees when you skip
3. Swing your arms at your side.
4. Step, hop. Step, hop. Step, hop.

Movement Exploration:
- What if you could draw on the floor with your feet? Create a picture while skipping.
- Create a forest with half the children being trees. The other children skip through the forest. Reverse roles.
- Who can skip in the yard trying to catch butterflies with a make-believe net?

- Can you skip forward, then diagonally?
- How many different ways can you move your body while you skip?
- Who can skip around the room giving your friends big smiles?
- Is it possible to skip while bringing your knees to a higher level?
- Show me how you can find a partner and skip while holding hands.
- Find another set of partners, and all of you hold hands and skip together.
- Discover if you can skip, stop, do a wiggle dance, skip, stop and wiggle.

Leaping—For Children Ages Five and Older
Teaching Cues for Leaping:

1. Take off from one foot and land on the other foot.
2. Strive for height and graceful flight.
3. Land lightly and relaxed.
4. Use your arms to help you leap.
5. Push off and reach.

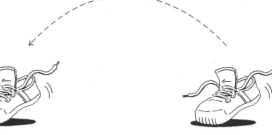

Movement Exploration:

- Suppose there is a huge mud puddle. Who can leap over it without getting muddy?
- Show me how you can leap as high in the air as possible.
- Can you leap over tall buildings like Superman?
- How many leaps will it take to get from one point to another?
- Who can lift their legs higher with each new leap?
- What ways can you leap with a partner?
- Is it possible for three people to stand side by side with the two end people running and the middle person leaping? Now have the end people leap and the middle person run.
- Try leaping over a make-believe pile of leaves.
- Discover the longest leap you can make.
- Show me how you can cross an imaginary stream by leaping from rock to rock.

IMPLEMENTATION STRATEGIES

Implementing a movement-based learning experience requires some preparation and forethought to ensure maximum participation with minimum risk. This may seem obvious to the reader, but the authors present them here for the benefit of new teachers and as a review for experienced teachers.

Clothing:

1. Please check that all sneakers are tied, and that they are on the proper feet for young children.
2. When possible, girls who are wearing a dress or skirt should be asked to slip on a pair of shorts to prepare for movement.
3. Be aware of dangling jewelry such as necklaces and bracelets.

Preparation of Playing Area:

1. In the classroom, all chair seats should be pushed under the desks.
2. Books and small obstacles should be removed from the floor and placed on tables or desks.

3. Larger obstacles should be moved to the sides of the room.
4. Check to make certain that the outdoor playing area is safe and free of debris, broken glass, and other harmful objects. Note if any child has allergies to bees or grass.
5. Specific boundaries as well as start and finish lines should be clearly marked and explained. Children should fully understand their limits.
6. Use a start and end signal. For example, "When the music begins you will start to move, and when the music stops, you must stop quickly." Other ending signals could include, "When the music stops, freeze wherever you are," "stay frozen in the exact body position you are in," "apply your brakes," or "pose for a photo." The teacher can use an imaginary camera to take photos.

Playing Safely:
1. For any chase and flee activity (i.e., tag-style game), children should be reminded of proper or gentle touches.
2. Children must listen to the teacher's directions and be respectful of the rules and of each other.
3. Arrange for proper spacing between groups. Children should not be running toward or into each other.
4. If children do not follow directions during an activity, stop the activity, and review your expectations.
5. Analyze the activity for possible safety problems. If you observe a risk of injury, stop the play and fix the problem.
6. Enforce rules about materials and equipment.
7. Pens, pencils, gum, lollipops, food, and drinks should be kept off the playing area.

MOVEMENT-BASED LEARNING FOR CHILDREN WITH SPECIAL NEEDS

With the increased acceptance of inclusion, and the need for every child to be taught in the least restrictive learning environment, both the teacher and the child can relate to the joy experienced through movement-based learning. The combination of using imitative and movement exploration permits more children to succeed through their natural ability to copy, imitate, and follow the teacher, or their desire to be expressive and respond in a variety of ways. Each movement-based learning experience can be used in a wide range of play spaces regardless of size, shape, or setting. However, it is suggested that all teachers become familiarized with each child's Individualized Education Program (IEP) or 504 Accommodation Plan to ensure that individually required accommodations are made prior to the implementation of any lesson. Discussions with parents and medical professionals may also be indicated.

Sample Teaching Considerations for Inclusion are as Follows:
A. Children with Visual Impairments
1. Brightly colored props and materials, as well as wall and floor markings should be used to assist in identifying segments of the playing area and boundaries.
2. Clear and succinct wording should be used in teacher directions.
3. Sound (e.g., music, whistle) can be used to indicate transitions and changes within the activity.
4. Provide a partner who can assist the child with visual impairments in following direction and movement.
5. Offer gentle physical guidance to help the child perform a variety of movement skills.
6. Consider using toys and dolls with moveable body parts to demonstrate and allow the child to feel various movement concepts.

B. Children with Hearing Impairments
1. The teacher should be situated near and facing the child to better facilitate the use of lip reading and sign language.
2. The lighting should be on the teacher, and not shining in the child's eyes.
3. The teacher should utilize visual aids such as cue cards, hand signals, and facial expressions.
4. Teachers may signify the beginning and ending of movement experiences with a flickering of lights.
5. All teachers should be aware of balance limitations due to the child's hearing loss.
6. The child with hearing impairments can also benefit by working with a partner.
7. The imitative approach allows for great success as the child with a hearing impairment follows posed movement phrases such as, "copy me, follow me, my turn... now your turn."

C. Children with Physical Disabilities
1. Teachers should consider greater space requirements needed for children who use wheelchairs.
2. It may be necessary to modify the distance traveled while performing a movement skill.
3. Teachers should consider utilizing lighter weight or varied shaped props to permit easier gripping and manipulation.
4. Immediately following the lesson, the teacher should allow time for readjustment of apparatus, such as braces, crutches, wheelchairs, and prosthetics.
5. All teachers should be well versed in the implications of the challenges each child faces, and their impact on the movement experience.
6. Be aware of physical signs or verbal cues indicating the child is experiencing the onset of difficulties symptomatic of the health impairment.
7. Recognize the onset of fatigue and the need to modify the next movement challenge to be less physically demanding.

D. Children with Emotional Disabilities
1. Teachers should use clear and consistent rules with this population, and state the student expectations and consequences.
2. Teachers should provide activities that encourage the child to express feelings and emotions.
3. Music can provide an additional prop to enhance self-expression and increase participation levels.
4. Children with emotional disabilities benefit from having a progression of learning experiences, beginning with the most simple and progressing to the more complex.
5. The child with behavioral or emotional issues who needs to avoid physical contact will benefit from individual learning experiences.
6. Whenever possible, remove any distractions and unnecessary obstacles and equipment from the playing area.

E. Children with Learning Disabilities
1. Children with learning disabilities benefit from short, concise instructions that can be repeated as necessary.
2. Teachers should be prepared to rephrase the instructions.
3. Utilizing positive reinforcement is a key component to successful participation.
4. The focus and direction of activities should be planned, keeping distractions to a minimum.

5. Teachers should always strive to be consistent in class management, behavior, and stating expectations.
6. All teachers should focus on achievements, regardless of how small, and use "powerful words to motivate students" cited in this chapter.

Finally, teachers striving for inclusion need to administer all movement learning experiences with a smile, patience, and an understanding of the unique challenges each child faces. A component of movement-based learning includes using positive reinforcement with regard to attempts and successes. This applies for all children, especially those who require self-esteem building, which is prevalent in children with special needs.

WAYS TO START AN ACTIVITY

In an average day, children use their senses to look or listen for indicators that signal them to start or stop activities. Children listen to the voices of older siblings and adults in charge. They respond to verbal cues and sounds to move to another activity, to lunch, to recess, to return to the classroom, and to pack up to go home. They look for traffic and hand signals to cross the street safely. They listen for automobile horns. Each day is filled with stimuli and forms of signals to indicate expected methods of behavior and response. In addition, children arrive home and do their homework, play, clean-up, wash up to have dinner, and get ready for bed and lights out. They respond to the love of their parents with mutual hugs and kisses.

In the gymnasium and in the classroom, children have also come to expect signals and sounds to assist them in the transition from one activity to the next. Movement-based learning also suggests utilizing signals for starting and stopping, and while making transitions from individual, partner, and whole-group learning. For example, experiences generally are started upon the initiation of the teacher's signal. This communication can be generated through sound, sight, or touch. Flickering lights, verbal cues, sounds, gentle touches, cue cards, music, or body movements easily convey the message that the teacher is ready to begin the activity. In movement exploration, verbal cues can be as simple as asking, "can you" or "who can...?" Using the imitative approach, the teacher can say, "Are you ready? (pause) go!" or "When I say three, we will start. Are you ready? One, two, three, (pause) go!"

Teachers can also use a prop or piece of equipment to start the activity. The teacher can explain to the children, "You can start when this handkerchief, paper, flag, or cloth leaves my hand. Are you ready?" Another idea would be for the teacher to raise his or her arm and explain to the children, "When I lower my arm and my hand touches my side, you can start. Are you ready?" The key is to ensure that the children understand the starting signal, and are focused on being ready to participate.

It is just as important for the teacher to have a signal to stop or end a learning experience. Children need to know when to stop. In the case of using music in the background, when the music is turned off, the children should know to stop. Some children respond to the word "stop" when spoken in a louder voice, a low pitched voice, or a softer voice, or an exaggerated "aaaannd (pause) stop!" It is also helpful to tell the children in advance whether the teacher expects them to stop and freeze in position, or sit where they are. Be aware that most children will take your words literally.

SAMPLE FORMATIONS FOR MOVEMENT-BASED LEARNING EXPERIENCES

Single-File Line: Children stand in back of one another, with eyes looking at the back of the head of the classmate in front of them. Teachers should be specific as to where the children should form a line. Please allow enough space for all children to fit on this line.

Side-by-Side Line: Children stand shoulder to shoulder. It is best to specify where you want them to stand (e.g., against the back wall or standing on the white line). If pushing or crowding occurs, ask the children to "stretch the line and make it longer."

Personal Space: Ask the children to find their own special spot in the playing area. This is called the child's personal or self space, where the child cannot touch someone else or an object.

Triangle: When forming a triangle, ask the children to form a group of three and face inward.

Circle with Teacher: When the teacher has the children organized in a circle formation, he or she should become part of the circle. If the teacher stands in the center of the circle, some children will only face the teacher's back.

One Body Length Apart: When the need for spacing between partners arises in an activity, ask the children to space themselves "one body length apart."

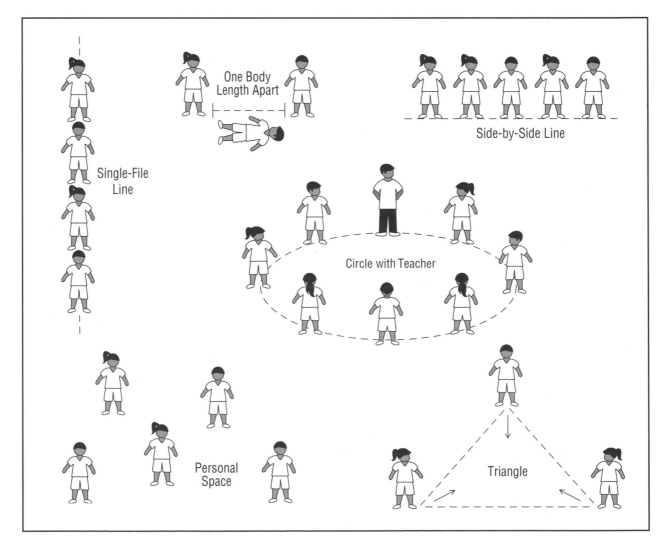

CREATIVE WAYS TO FORM GROUPS

There are many ways to assist children in becoming a part of a larger group. It is important to keep in mind the sensitive nature of younger children. With their boundless energy and excitement for play, they tend to forget assigned numbers or colors. Teachers may find success in many of the proven techniques below.

Finding a partner

The teacher should be sensitive to children who are consistently unable to find a partner to avoid the "last one chosen" stigma by using the following techniques:

- Ask children to find someone who has their same color hair, eyes, or clothing.
- Invite the children to find someone who likes the same flavor ice cream.
- Tell the children to find someone who has the same number of syllables in his or her first name.
- Tell the children, "When I say go, please find a partner. Are you ready? Ready, get set, (pause) go!"
- Play music and have the children smile and greet one another while moving throughout the playing area. When the music stops, the children who last greeted one another become partners.
- Request that each child find a partner who was born in the same season.
- Ask children to circulate and find a partner. Any child who does not have a partner is considered "lost" and moves to the teacher who is in charge of the "lost and found" department. The teacher then pairs any lost children, and if there is only one child, the child selects whatever group he or she wants.

Creating Small Groups

- Ask partners to join another set of partners to make a group of four.
- Distribute a deck of playing cards. Groups of four are formed in terms of having the same number. Flash cards also provide opportunities for finding others with the same picture, color, number, or letter.
- In classrooms where children sit at colored tables, children can be divided by tables.
- Teachers can use Popsicle sticks (or slips of paper) with the names of the child written on each one and stored in one container. The teacher then pulls out four sticks from the container to form a group.

Creating Two Large Groups

- Two differently colored pom-poms can be placed in a container or lunch bag. Each child selects a pom-pom. Other items such as colored plastic jacks, colored popsicle sticks, stickers, or small plastic figurines work well.
- Props of assorted shapes, colors, or sizes (e.g., bean bags, yarn, styrofoam, or wood blocks) being used for the movement learning experience can be used as well. See the list of sample props for movement-based learning experiences later in this chapter.
- Using a side-by-side line, ask the children to either take a giant step forward or a

giant step backward. Those who moved forward are in the first group, and those who took their step back are in the second group.

- Each child decides quietly whether to be a cow who says "Moo" or a cat who says "Meow." Children walk throughout the playing area, creating their animal sounds. Once all the animals find each other, the cows go to one side of the playing area and the cats move to the opposite side.

- Children are asked to close their eyes and either raise their hands or keep their hands to the side.

- The "ZZZZIP line" has the teacher moving quickly through the children, while saying the magic word "ZZZZIP." Children on each side of the zip line form a group.

- Please keep in mind that most movement-based learning experiences do not require an exact number of children within each group.

UTILIZING PROPS AND EQUIPMENT

Props can add a sense of realism to learning experiences for both the teacher and the child. When using the imitative and the movement exploration approach, children are instantly more motivated to become physically active when props are included. With a little thought, the teacher can easily spark the child's imagination. This could be as simple as using a storybook with pictures, small plastic animals or figurines, or still pictures of common objects. Learning experiences involving props can be conducted in the classroom, the multipurpose room, the gymnasium, and outdoors. To explore a few of the materials that are easily obtained, the following identifies how sample props are used in a lesson focusing on the beach. The actual individual/partner and whole-group movement experiences can be found in Chapter Five.

Primary Learning Objective Focusing on the Beach

To provide a learning environment for children to reinforce academic concepts while participating in creative and enjoyable beach-related experiences.

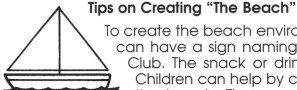

Tips on Creating "The Beach"

To create the beach environment, the entrance to the room or play area can have a sign naming the area, (Name of school or facility) Beach Club. The snack or drink area can be called "The Slimy Clam Bar." Children can help by creating murals, posters, and drawings reflecting the beach. These can be used as wall decorations. Sea life and beach-related cut-outs, magazine and newspaper photos, travel brochures, and posters can complete the scene. Background music, relating to the beach, can be played during snacks and activities. Music may include sound tracks of ocean waves, seagulls, whales, steel drums, and movie songs pertaining to the beach. Teachers can choose from a variety of books having stories with scenes taking place at the beach. They can also invent stories to create the setting for an activity, and dress the part.

Obtaining Props for the Beach

A neighborhood provides a wealth of supplies for recreating a beach. Large free standing cut-outs are found at store chains, fast food

restaurants, movie theaters, music and video stores, and travel agencies. Most are discarded or donated at the discretion of the store manager. Exploring local garage sales, bazaars, flea markets, and discount stores may be the key to finding items such as music, books, beach balls, beach toys, sunglasses, and craft supplies. Many card stores discard unsold seasonal cards, wrapping paper, and paper goods. Posters can also be found at theaters, music and video stores, museums, aquariums, and pet stores. Party good stores carry beach-related paper goods, party favors, sunglasses, sun hats, beach balls, and music. Travel agencies are great sources for posters, maps, and brochures. Toy stores sell plastic fish, turtles, shellfish, sunglasses, beach balls, books, and craft supplies. Pictures can be downloaded from the Internet and used for decorations or learning tools. A trip to the beach to collect seashells and driftwood is highly recommended.

Snack Time at "The Slimy Clam Bar"

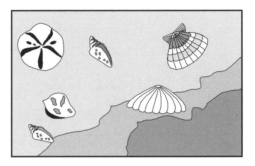

Healthy snacks can also be a consideration. The items may include something as simple as Goldfish crackers. A peach can be called a "Beach Peach," and a slice of watermelon becomes a "Watermelon Wave." Banana Boats are easily made using a banana with the center cut out to form a boat. The center of the banana is then filled with raisins, nuts, and/or grapes. For a healthy lunch, a Tuna Boat is created by filling a hot dog roll with tuna salad. To complete the effect, a toothpick is speared through a slice of cheese to make a cheese sail. Dessert considerations include low-fat cupcakes decorated with blue icing and graham cracker crumbs as sand. These cupcakes can be called, "Fun in the Sun Cupcakes," or the children can decorate frozen yogurt with fresh fruit to create a "Sun Day."

In addition to the movement-based learning experiences found in Chapter Five, children ages three through eight also benefit from guest speakers who have expertise in beach-related content. These might include lifeguards, marine biologists, or owners of local pet stores or aquariums who could bring live fish and sea creatures. In contrast, teachers can provide a quiet area where the children can lie down on beach blankets while listening to the sounds of ocean waves and sea gulls. Relaxation and creative visualization techniques can be used during this time. This is an effective method to calm children after a very busy day. If field trips are available, a trip to the beach provides opportunities for digging for buried treasure and creating sand sculptures. Children can also visit a local pet store or aquarium. The extent that teachers use props is only limited by one's imagination.

SAMPLE PROPS AND EQUIPMENT FOR MOVEMENT-BASED LEARNING

CLASSROOM ITEMS

- Chairs • Chalk • Carpet Squares
- Classroom Blocks • Card Table
- Finger or Hand Puppets
- Desks • Books • Wooden Blocks
- Pictures • Magic Box

COMMUNITY ITEMS

- Planks of Lumber
- Tires • Ladder • Barrels
- PVC Pipe • Rain Gutters
- Saw Horse • Cable Spools
- Packing Crates
- Road Signs • Travel Posters

HOUSEHOLD ITEMS

- Cardboard Boxes • Shoe Boxes
- Paper Plates • Paper Hats
- Bowls • Paper Bags • Sponges
- Pillows • Old Tube Socks
- Tin Foil • Bed Sheets • Blankets
- Newspaper • Ropes • Balloons
- Paper Towel Tubes
- Rolls of Gift Wrap • Water Hose
- Toilet Paper Tubes
- Plastic Bottles—empty and clean

- Mattress • Mirrors • Maps
- Plastic Buckets • Bubble Wrap
- Bicycle Inner Tubes
- Stuffed Animals • Pinwheel
- Flash Cards—animals, colors, letters, numbers
- Music • Sound Effects Music
- Homemade Rhythm Instruments
- Dress up clothing
- Mobile

ART SUPPLIES

- Art Paper
- Construction Paper
- Crepe Paper
- Styrofoam
- Dowel Sticks
- Popsicle Sticks
- String • Tape
- Clay • Ribbon

EQUIPMENT

- Bean Bags (available in colors, numbers, animal shapes, or can be homemade)
- Hoops • Jump Ropes
- Tumbling Mats • Cones
- Floor Spots • Frisbees
- Burlap Sacks

OUTDOOR ITEMS

- Rocks
- Cut Grass
- Sand • Bales of Hay
- Bags of Leaves • Branches

POWERFUL WORDS TO MOTIVATE CHILDREN

"Children don't care how much you know, until they know how much you care."

Movement-based learning relies on teachers praising the children after new skills are introduced, or after a successful partner or whole-group learning experience. Children appreciate kind words, and knowing that they have been noticed for good work and extra effort. To help increase the child's level of self-esteem, teachers need to develop a repertoire of encouraging words and phrases that extend beyond the phrase "good job." The following suggested phrases or expressions are intended to help fill this void.

Individual Learning Experiences

"You did it!"
"I'm so proud of you!"
"Let me shake your hand."
"Congratulations kiddo!"
"You've got it now!"
"Good for you."
"You should really feel proud of yourself."
"You really are very good at that."
"I admire your talent."

"You made that look easy."
"See what you can accomplish if you try."
"How do you feel now?"
"I knew you could do it."
"That just took my breath away."
"Instant replay!"
"I love your razzle dazzle smile!"
"I'm proud of you for trying."

"In my eyes, you are a winner."
"I appreciate your help."
"I like the way you thought of that."
"I admire your determination."
"Believe in yourself; I believe in you."
"You almost have it."
"I can tell you're trying very hard"
"Wow! With a little practice, look what you can do."

Partner Learning Experiences

"You can do it!"
"Great going!"
"Way to go!"
"Very nice!"
"Wonderful!"
"Well done!"
"Wow!"

"Perfect!"
"I like that."
"Wow! ...The dynamic duo!"
"I admire your skills."
"I'm impressed!"
"Thank you!"

"I wish I had my camera."
"Absolutely perfect!"
"I can tell you've both been practicing."
"Now that's what I call perfect."
"Together you can make it happen."

"You're getting better each time."
"Much better."
"Nice try!"
"You made that look easy."
"You two are terrific."
"I like how you share."
"What a great idea!"

Group Learning Experiences

"Super duper!"
"Fantastic!"
"Excellent!"
"Outstanding!"
"Amazing!"
"I love it!"
"Outrageous!"

"Magnificent!"
"Awesome!"
"Terrific!"
"Tremendous!"
"Yes!"
"Good thinking!"

"You almost have it!"
"That's incredible!"
"Marvelous!"
"Remarkable!"
"This is great!"
"You have really outdone yourselves."
"That's the best ever!"

"Now that's what I call creative thinking."
"That's more like it."
"Your group effort is astonishing."
"That's the way!"
"This is what I call group effort."

Please keep in mind that using a variety of encouraging words will make each child feel special. The delivery is in the smile and the expressive way in which the phrase is spoken. Praise brings a smile to each child's face, and conveys that the teacher cares.

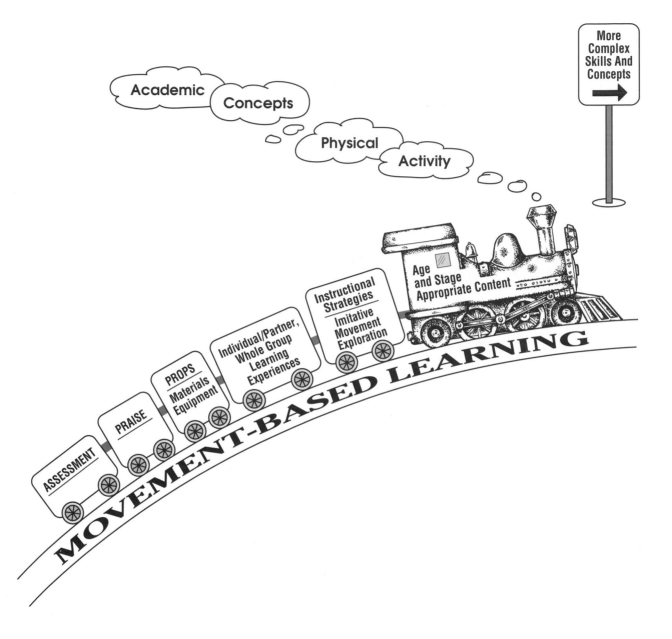

Enhancing the Child's Movement
Vocabulary and Language Arts Skills

Enhancing the Child's Movement Vocabulary and Language Arts Skills

Unlike many resources that reinforce academic concepts through movement activities, movement-based learning uses classroom content to expand the child's movement repertoire. This use of academic concepts to enhance the child's movement abilities should appeal to classroom teachers who desire a fresh approach to meeting learning standards. This is especially true if they have neglected to use the physical domain in their instruction due to a lack of available resources. Using academic concepts should also assist the physical education teacher's desire to expand the child's "movement vocabulary." From the child's perspective, he or she is simply using the information experienced in the classroom to participate in fun and physically active movement challenges.

THE ALPHABET, BODY SHAPES, AND SUBSTANCES LEARNING EXPERIENCES

The first series of learning experiences are devoted to classroom concepts that focus on the alphabet. Children can expand their understanding that each letter in the alphabet can be used to create a movement word (see "Movement Alphabet A-Z"), and they learn that they can use their bodies to create letters in the alphabet. Still other learning experiences in this section appeal to the child's love for rhyming words and active movement.

These challenges are followed by a series of activities that generate the children's interest in learning about shapes and substances, and how we can use our understanding of these objects and living things to move in creative ways (see "Shapes the Child's Body Can Make"). Each learning experience is designed to use the child's understanding of the academic concept, and then how to use this new understanding to enhance the child's movement response.

MOVEMENT NARRATIVE LEARNING EXPERIENCES

By a child's third birthday, most children have obtained a variety of language and intellectual skills, have acquired specific likes and dislikes, are more adept at manipulating objects, and have been introduced to numerous settings. The ability to demonstrate a variety of movement skills has allowed the child to independently explore the environment without adult intervention. It is not, however, totally clear why some children are more highly imaginative and creative than others. Some educators believe that imaginative children are simply born, and others think that creativity is a product of the young child's physical environment and exposure to a wide variety of stimulation. It is generally known that these qualities can be encouraged and fostered in children ages three through eight years. Furthermore, it is critical to do so or risk the chance that the child's creative abilities may be impaired later, or even destroyed.

Therefore, the second series of activities focus on the use of movement narratives. Movement narratives are one means by which physical educators, classroom teachers, and dance educators can introduce fictional characters, settings, and events to expand the child's imagination and creativity, love for stories, and language arts skills. In the cognitive or intellectual domain, narratives increase the child's movement vocabulary, language skills, and love for words that remind him or her of sounds. In the affective/social domain, narratives help the child to understand how different family members and people react to situations and interact with each other. They also indicate

MOVEMENT ALPHABET A-Z

Challenge the children to perform the following stretching movements:

"A" is for the Air. Who can *take* three deep breaths of air?

"B" is for Bouncing. Can you *bounce* like a rubber ball?

"C" is for Curling. Who can *curl* their body into a round shape?

"D" is for Dodging. Can you *dodge* to one side and then to the other side?

"E" is for Exploring. Pretend to *explore* a long, dark cave.

"F" is for Fun. Show me how your body *moves* when you are having fun.

"G" is for Grip. Can you *curl* your fingers and *make* a tight grip?

"H" is for Hug. *Give* yourself a great big hug.

"I" is for Inflate. Let's pretend to *blow* and *inflate* a giant balloon.

"J" is for Jump. Try to *jump* upward and *touch* the ceiling.

"K" is for Kick. Show me how you can *kick* an imaginary ball with your foot.

"L" is for Lower. How slowly can you *lower* your body to the floor?

"M" is for Muscle. Try to *stretch* your arm muscles and *make* them long.

"N" is for Narrow. *Show* me a tall, narrow shape.

"O" is for Over. Pretend to *step* over a giant hole in the ground.

"P" is for Plod. How would you *walk* while *plodding* through deep snow?

"Q" is for Quick. Can you *move* your hands quickly at the sides of the body?

"R" is for Roll. Is it possible to *create* a long shape and *roll* along the floor?

"S" is for Swim. Show me how you can pretend to *swim* with your arms.

"T" is for Tip-Toe. *Stretch* high into the sky on your tiptoes.

"U" Is for Upward. Make-belleve you are a kite *soaring* upward.

"V" is for Vibrate. Can you *rock, shake,* and *vibrate* like a giant machine?

"W" is for Wiggle. What ways can you *wiggle* your fingers?

"X" is for X-ray. *Point* to a bone in your hand.

"Y" is for Yank. Show me how you can *yank* an imaginary rope.

"Z" is for Zigzag. Is it possible to *skip* in a zigzag pattern?

SHAPES THE CHILD'S BODY CAN MAKE...

• round • oval • narrow • stretched • small • tall • short
• twisted • triangle • square • thin • pointed • wide • little • angular • big
• curved • sharp • circle • rectangle • flat • long • curled • tiny
• crooked • gigantic • straight • box • diamond • skinny

that people like different things and have different viewpoints. This domain also provides opportunities for children to begin to take the perspective of others in simple ways, such as acting very brave or frightened. These actions are one of the earliest steps toward developing empathy for other people, and experimenting with adult roles of power and control. Finally, within the psychomotor/physical domain, narratives offer numerous opportunities for the child to demonstrate a wide variety of movement skills in an environment that encourages imaginative responses and creative expression. In short, movement narratives satisfy all three domains of learning.

The Three Domains of Learning

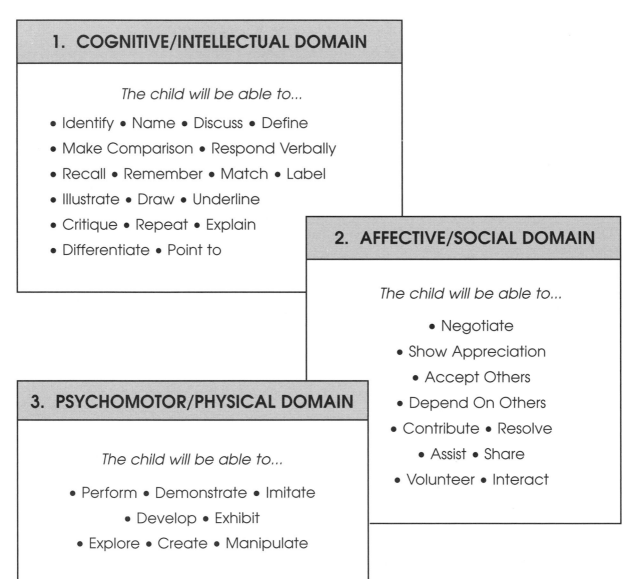

1. COGNITIVE/INTELLECTUAL DOMAIN

The child will be able to...

- Identify • Name • Discuss • Define
- Make Comparison • Respond Verbally
- Recall • Remember • Match • Label
- Illustrate • Draw • Underline
- Critique • Repeat • Explain
- Differentiate • Point to

2. AFFECTIVE/SOCIAL DOMAIN

The child will be able to...

- Negotiate
- Show Appreciation
- Accept Others
- Depend On Others
- Contribute • Resolve
- Assist • Share
- Volunteer • Interact

3. PSYCHOMOTOR/PHYSICAL DOMAIN

The child will be able to...

- Perform • Demonstrate • Imitate
- Develop • Exhibit
- Explore • Create • Manipulate

IMPLEMENTING NARRATIVES

The following information should assist the teacher in implementing movement narratives:

1. Foster and develop the child's mental picture of the situation by reading the narrative slowly and with enthusiasm. Some teachers and parents mistakenly assume that complex toys and elaborate costumes are needed to inspire the child's imaginative abilities. They overlook the fact that imaginative qualities stem from the child's ability to perform creative thinking and simple problem solving. Allow a moment for the child to visualize the desired movement response. Encourage the child to "think before you move."

2. Assist the child in learning to interact with peers in a social way. Discuss the inter-personal skills needed to take turns, lead and follow, share, and cooperate with one another or even a sibling at home.

3. Use the imitative approach for those young children that may have difficulty interpreting all of the action words. This is possible by demonstrating the correct way to perform a movement, and by narrowing the child's focus to one action or expression at a time. The teacher would then allow the young children to complete the skill or action before moving on to the next sentence.

4. Adapt or modify your voice to take on the voice of different characters presented in each narrative.

5. Identify and praise those individuals who are expressing their feeling freely and are actively involved.

6. Talk about the different movements demonstrated throughout the narrative. Which movements helped the character to accomplish the goal of the story? What actions were used to show how each body was moving?

7. Suggest other ways that the narrative could have ended, and ask the children to physically demonstrate how each might have looked.

8. Always praise the children's efforts and creativity when they successfully complete the narrative. Assess the child's understanding of the action words and movement abilities to see that learning has taken place.

THE GREAT ALPHABET HUNT

Primary Learning Objective: The children will imitate movements common to objects and things that begin with each letter of the alphabet.

Materials or Equipment: None

Formation: Children are in their personal spaces.

Individual or Partner Learning Experience:
The teacher presents the following:

Explain that today is the day of the Great Alphabet Hunt. The Great Alphabet Hunt takes place every (fall, winter or spring). The children's task is to use their imagination to move with each letter of the alphabet. Explain that some of the objects are very large, and some are very small. The children must put the imaginary objects into a magic sack. This magic sack will let them carry all the objects at the same time.

A – IS FOR APPLE
Since the apple tree is very tall, you will need to reach upwards as high as you can. Now *stretch* up on your tip-toes and *grab* for an apple. When you reach the apple, *pull* it down and *place* it in your sack.

B – IS FOR BICYCLE
A bicycle needs to be pedaled. Use your legs and pretend to *pedal* a bicycle before you put it in the sack.

C – IS FOR COW
To get a cow's attention, you need to sound like a cow. Can you do that?

D – IS FOR DINOSAUR.
Dinosaurs are very large and heavy animals. To catch a dinosaur, *move* quietly and slowly on your hands and feet.

E – IS FOR EGG
Eggs break very easily. You will need to carefully lift them from a nest so they do not break. Pretend you are *protecting* the eggs with your arms.

F – IS FOR FROG
Frogs live in ponds and jump from lily pad to lily pad. To catch a frog, make-believe you are *following* a frog across the pond.

G – IS FOR GUITAR
Guitars have strings to make music. Can you *strum* a tune? We can all play together. Ready? One, two, three.

H – IS FOR HORSE
When horses move very quickly, we call the action galloping. See if you can *gallop* in a circle.

I – IS FOR ICE CREAM
Ice cream is very cold until it begins to melt. Can you make your body *shiver* like the temperature of ice cream? Slowly *melt* to the floor.

J – IS FOR JELL-O
Jell-O wiggles and jiggles. Show me that you can *wiggle* and *jiggle*.

K – IS FOR KANGAROO
Kangaroos carry their babies in a pouch, and they jump using their back legs. How high can you *jump*?

L – IS FOR LASSO
Lassos are special ropes that cowboys and cowgirls use. They *twirl* them high over their heads and at the side of their bodies. What kinds of things can you do with a lasso?

M – IS FOR MONKEY
Monkeys *climb* and *swing* on vines, and *jump* from tree to tree. How would you *act* if you were a monkey?

N – IS FOR NOODLE
Before noodles are cooked, they are very stiff. After they are cooked, they are limp and wiggly. Who can show me what happens to a noodle when it is cooked?

O – IS FOR OCTOPUS
An octopus lives in the water and has eight tentacles. Tentacles are like our arms and legs. Make-believe your legs and arms are tentacles.

P – IS FOR PARACHUTE
People use parachutes when they jump out of planes. Parachutes help them to float to the ground safely. Show me how you can *jump* and then *float* to the ground.

Q – IS FOR QUACK
Ducks quack as they waddle. Show me how you can quack and *waddle.*

R – IS FOR ROBOT
Robots are made of metal and use jerky motions when they walk. Who can show me how a robot *walks*?

S – IS FOR SNAKE
Snakes do not have arms or legs so they must slither on the ground by wiggling their body. Make-believe that you are a snake.

T – IS FOR TOP
Tops spin around and around. Let's all *spin* like a top without falling down.

U – IS FOR UMBRELLA
Umbrellas help to keep us dry when it rains. Please *pick* up one umbrella, *open* and *close* it, and *put* it in your sack.

V – IS FOR VOLCANO
Volcanoes are mountains that contain a very hot liquid inside. When this liquid gets too hot, it suddenly shoots up from the top of the volcano. Is it possible to *explode* like a volcano?

W – IS FOR WORM
Worms look like very small snakes, and they live in the dirt. To find a worm, show me how you would *dig* a hole.

X – IS FOR XYLOPHONE
Xylophones are musical instruments that you play by using two sticks. Before you place it in the sack, let's try to *play* a song. One, two, three.

Y – IS FOR YO-YO
Yo-yos *move* up and down on a string. Imagine you are a yo-yo.

Z – IS FOR ZIPPER
Zippers help us to close our coats, pants, or shirts. Zippers also move up and down. Show me how you can *close* an imaginary coat.

Wonderful!!!! You have completed the Great Alphabet Hunt.

Creative Closure:

1. Who can move like your most favorite object or living thing?

2. I hope that you remembered to place the objects in your magic sack. Next year, the Great Alphabet Hunt will begin again with new objects to find. Before we leave, please empty your sack into the box in the center of the play area so that others will find these special objects someday when they play the Great Alphabet Hunt.

ALPHABET ROCK AND ROLL

Primary Learning Objective: The children will perform actions that coincide with words for each letter of the alphabet.

Materials or Equipment: None

Formation: Children are in their personal spaces.

Individual or Partner Learning Experience:
The teacher presents the following:

We got the moves from A to Z,
Clap your hands and *stomp* your feet.

We got the moves from A to Z,
Come and make some moves with me.

A is for alligator, *chomp, chomp, chomp,*
B is for bear, *tramping* with a thump.

C is for cat, *chasing* a mouse,
D is for dog, *crawling* into his house.

E is for elephant, *eating* peanuts from
my hand,
F is for fish, *plunging* toward the sand.

G is for ghost that makes us
tremble and *shake,*
H is for *happy* faces we can make.

I is for inchworm, *creeping* along
my arm,
J is for jolly, *rolling* pigs on the farm.

K is for kite, *flying* in the sky,
L is for lizards, *leaping* high.

M is for mouse, *sitting quiet* as can be,
N is for bird, *chirping* in a nest in a tree.

O is for octopus, *wrapped* in a ball,
P is for peacock, *strutting* proud and tall.

Q is for the quickness of a *jumping*
kangaroo,
R is for rooster, *crowing* cock-a-doodle-do.

S is for slimy, *slithering* snake,
T is for tortoise, *strolling* by the lake.

U is for looking upward to find a shooting
star,
V is for the vroom, vroom, vroom of a
race car.

W is for the *whirling* winds of a cyclone,
X is for the circus animals, *dancing* to the
xylophone.

Y is for yaks, *plodding* two by two,
Z is for zebra, *zipping* through the zoo.

Creative Closure:

1. What object or thing challenged you to move the most?

2. Can you think of another way to move to your favorite letter?

ALPHABET SOUP

Primary Learning Objective: The children will exhibit a variety of expressive feelings while being moderately physically active.

Materials or Equipment: None

Formation: Children are in their personal spaces.

Individual or Partner Learning Experience:
The teacher presents the following:

Once upon a time, in a *round shaped* bowl,
lived the letters of the alphabet, and fun was their goal.

The mischievous letters liked to *splash* and *swirl*.
They *gracefully swam* and *merrily twirled*.

The A's were *adorable,* the B's *bounced* high.
The C's *crept* and *crawled,* while the D's *darted* by.

The E's *eeked* at the *fun* and *friendly* F's.
The G's *galloped,* the H's *hid,* but the I's were not *impressed*.

The *jittery* J's *jumped* about, as the K's *kicked* the air
and the L's all *leaped* out.

The M's *marched mightily* but the *nervous* N's never knew, that
the O's obviously *jumped* over the *pretty* P's and the *quiet* Q's.

The R's *rested* and *relaxed,* as the S's *swayed shyly*.
The *tense* T's took turns *treading* water *wildly*.

The U's *hid* underneath an umbrella.
The V's *vigorously vanished*. The W's *wandered* near each other.

The X's explained to the *yawning* Y's, that the Z's are all
Zigzagging to keep themselves alive.

The small *scary* boy with the spoon wants a treat,
and I am *afraid* it is us that he wants to *eat*.

The alphabet letters were *frightened* as they *scurried* around.
What will they do, if they are found?

The boy *drifted* closer with a *smile* on his face.
He then *lunged* for the cupboard in a *quick* and *excited* pace.

As he *reached* up they *noticed,* a box he did *lift*.
To their great *relief,* it was a cereal box of Alphabits!

Creative Closure:

1. Select three different movements that show me you are happy.

2. Find other ways to show me that you are feeling friendly.

MY MOVEMENT ALPHABET

Primary Learning Objective: Children will use their bodies to move like objects, starting with a specific alphabet letter.

Materials or Equipment: None

Formation: Children are in their personal spaces.

Individual or Partner Learning Experience:
The teacher presents the following:

1. Each letter of the alphabet can be used to represent items or things. Let's use our bodies to move to different objects beginning with alphabet letters.

— A —
- Ants *scurrying*
- Airplanes *soaring*
- Astronauts *floating*
- Apes *swinging*

— B —
- Birds *flying*
- Bees *buzzing*
- Balloons *inflating*
- Butterflies *fluttering*
- Bubbles *bursting*
- Balls *bouncing*
- Bats *swinging*
- Buffalos *stampeding*

— C —
- Clocks *ticking*
- Cats *arching*
- Chicks *chirping*
- Cars *racing*

(Crabs)
- Crabs *walking*
- Camels *plodding*
- Crows *flying*
- Crocodiles *crawling*

— D —
- Ducks *waddling*
- Dogs *crunching*
- Drums *beating*
- Dancers *twirling*
- Dolphins *leaping*
- Deer *running*
- Donkeys *plodding*

— E —
- Elephants *stomping*
- Eskimos *building*
- Elbows *bending*
- Eagles *soaring*

— F —
- Fans *spinning*
- Fish *swimming*
- Feet *stamping*
- Frogs *jumping*

— G —
- Gerbils *scurrying*
- Goats *kicking*
- Geese *flying*
- Goldfish *swimming*
- Gophers *digging*

— H —
- Hammers *pounding*
- Hands *clapping*
- Hippopotami *splashing*
- Helicopters *hovering*

— I —
- Ice skates *sliding*
- Ice *melting*

— J —
- Jets *soaring*
- Jump ropes *turning*
- Jaguars *searching*
- Jellyfish *floating*

— K —
- Kittens *stretching*
- Keys *turning*
- Knots *twisting*
- Kites *soaring*

— L —
- Lions *pouncing*
- Leopards *stalking*
- Lambs *prancing*
- Lungs *expanding*

— M —
- Mice *scampering*
- Mops *swishing*
- Motorcycles *speeding*
- Machines *vibrating*
- Muscles *stretching*

— N —
- Neon lights *flashing*
- Nightingales *flying*

— O —
- Owls *hooting*
- Oak trees *swaying*

— P —
- Pigs *rolling*
- Popcorn *popping*
- Pinwheels *twirling*
- Penguins *shuffling*
- People *hugging*

— Q —
- Quails *cooing*

— R —
- Rabbits *jumping*
- Roosters *strutting*
- Rhinoceroses *charging*
- Reindeer *prancing*

— S —
- Snails *slithering*
- Sleds *dashing*
- Sailors *scrubbing*
- Squirrels *scampering*
- Spiders *crawling*
- Seals *clapping*
- Scorpions *stinging*

— T —
- Tigers *charging*
- Tails *wagging*
- Trains *trudging*
- Trees *swaying*
- Turkeys *trotting*
- Trout *swimming*

— U —
- Umbrellas *opening*

— V —
- Vehicles *zooming*
- Vines *climbing*
- Vultures *circling*

— W —
- Water *dripping*
- Whales *diving*
- Woodcutters *chopping*
- Wolves *howling*
- Woodpeckers *pecking*
- Worms *wiggling*
- Wheels *turning*

— X Y Z —
- Yo-Yos *rising* and *lowering*
- Yachts *sailing*
- Zebras *galloping*

Creative Closure:
1. Show me how you can trace your favorite letter in the air.
2. Invent a new way of moving to that letter.

ALPHABET BODIES

Primary Learning Objective: The children are challenged to create alphabet letters by using their bodies to form lines and half circles.

Materials or Equipment: One large poster containing the letters of the alphabet, displayed at a height that permits all children to see the letters clearly. The dots on each letter indicate where each child's head can be positioned.

Formation: Children are working in sets of partners, trios, and groups of four.

Individual or Partner Learning Experience:
The teacher presents the following:

1. People learn to print alphabet letters by drawing straight lines and half circles.

2. Who can demonstrate a long, thin, narrow shape at a low level? These shapes are needed to make the lines in alphabet letters.

3. Select a partner, buddy, or pal to form three different alphabet letters at a low level.

Whole-Group Learning Experience:
ALPHABET BODIES: Reorganize the children into groups of four. Ask each group of four to select and form one alphabet letter. Complete the activity by having the class, as a whole, use their bodies to spell out the "word of the week." Write the word in large letters for all to see, and review what the word means.

Creative Closure:

1. Which letters were the most difficult to create with our bodies?

2. Can you think of a three-letter word that you could create with a trio that means to be happy (joy or fun)?

IN YOUR MIND HOPSCOTCH I

NASPE
Learning Standard
#1, #2

Primary Learning Objective: The children will use their auditory skills to identify the rhyming words that coincide with the number of times needed to jump.

Materials or Equipment: None

Formation: Children are in their personal spaces.

Individual or Partner Learning Experience:
The teacher presents the following:

1. Jump up and down if you have ever seen a hopscotch pattern. After I read a rhyme, show me you can respond by shouting out the answer to the rhyme, and by jumping the correct number of times in your personal spaces.

An old game, we have made new,
This is what you need to do.

You will have fun while you learn
Words and numbers with each turn.

To play, you jump the number of a word that rhymes.
Like, when you hear the word "tree," you *jump* three times.

One
When you *shake* hands with someone,
Or *feel* the bones in your skeleton,
You only *jump* _____ (one).

Two
If you *paddle* down a river in a canoe,
Or skip to your neighborhood zoo,
You *jump* _____ (two).

Three
Can you *buzz* about like a bee?
Or *swing* from a branch like a monkey,
You *jump* _____ (three).

Four
Can you make-believe to use a broom to *sweep* a floor,
Or *stamp* and *stomp* like a heavy dinosaur,
You *jump* _____ (four).

Five
Who can *point* to an object that is alive?
Or pretend to *leap* from an airplane and skydive,
You *jump* _____ (five).

(cont.)

Six

If you see ants *scurrying* at picnics,
Or can pretend you are a magician doing *tricks*,
You *jump* _____ (six).

Seven

If you can *tell* a joke like a comedian,
Or imagine you can *crawl* like a baby in a playpen,
You *jump* _____ (seven).

Eight

If your body is strong and you *feel* great,
Or *stand* in a long line and have to wait,
You *jump* _____ (eight).

Nine

If you *fly* on an airline,
Or *give* someone a valentine,
You jump _____ (nine).

Ten

If you take a deep breath of oxygen,
Or visit a bear at home in its den,
You *jump* _____ (ten).

End

That's all. You are done.
Yes, this game is easy and fun.
Oops, you need to *jump* _____ (one)!

Creative Closure:

1. Who can think of two words that rhyme?

2. What if I said vine and gold mine. Who can jump _____?

IN YOUR MIND HOPSCOTCH II

Primary Learning Objective: The children will use their auditory skills to identify the rhyming words that coincide with the number of times needed to hop.

Materials or Equipment: None

Formation: Children are in their personal spaces.

Individual or Partner Learning Experience:
The teacher presents the following:

1. Hop up and down if you have ever seen a hopscotch pattern. After I read a rhyme, show me you can respond by shouting out the answer to the rhyme, and by hopping the correct number of times in your personal space.

An old game, we have made new,
This is what you need to do.

You will have fun while you learn
Words and numbers with each turn.

To play, you hop the number of a word that rhymes.
Like, when you hear the word "glue," you *hop* two times.

One
When you *rise* in the morning and see the sun,
Have fun, taking your dog for a *run,*
Watch the sunset on the horizon,
Keep *playing* a game until you have won,
You only *hop* _____ (one).

Two
If you *wear* the color blue,
Wash your hair with shampoo,
Can *tie* your shoe,
Or have *played* Peek-a-Boo,
You *hop* _____ (two).

Three
With your eyes you can *see,*
When your friends *visit,* you have company,
You and me *becomes* we,
Together we can make an important discovery,
You *hop* _____ (three).

Four
You don't need to keep score,
If you *walk* through a door,
Or *shop* at a store,
Row a boat with an oar,
You *hop* _____ (four).

(cont.)

Five

You *enter* a car and go for a *drive,*
Watch a swimmer take a *dive,*
Or a *swarm* of bees in a hive,
Travel until you arrive,
You *hop* _____ (five).

Six

If you *see* a building of bricks,
Watch soccer players having kicks,
Play pick up sticks,
See children *hopping* up and down on pogo sticks,
You *hop* _____ (six).

Seven

Do you know a boy named Kevin,
Or maybe someone named Devon,
You do not need to *hop* to eleven,
You *hop* _____ (seven).

Eight

If you are *late,*
Like to skate,
Eat from a plate,
Shiver from cold until you *vibrate,*
You *hop* _____ (eight).

Nine

If you are in a forest, and *see* a pine,
Can *tie* a knot from twine,
Or *draw* a line,
Make a design,
You *hop* _____ (nine).

Ten

You *know* a boy, whose name is Ben, Ken, or Glen,
Write a letter to a friend with a pen,
Be a good citizen,
Ride horses with an equestrian,
You *hop* _____ (ten).

End

That's all. You are done.
Yes, this game is easy and fun.
Oops, you need to *hop* _____ (one).

Creative Closure:

1. What body parts do you use to help you hop?

2. Who can hold a partner's hand and hop throughout the playing area?

IN YOUR MIND HOPSCOTCH III

Primary Learning Objective: The children will use their auditory skills to identify the rhyming words that coincide with the number of times needed to move in a variety of ways.

Materials or Equipment: None

Formation: Children are in their personal spaces.

Individual or Partner Learning Experience:
The teacher presents the following:

1. Wiggle and shake if you have ever seen a hopscotch pattern. After I read the rhyme, show me how you can respond by shouting out the answer to the rhyme, and performing the specified movement throughout general space.

An old game, we have made new.
This is what you need to do.

You will have fun while you learn
Words and numbers with each turn.

To play, you hop the number of a word that rhymes.
Like, when you hear the word "knee," you *move* three times.

One
If you are nice to everyone,
And *smile* and *laugh* when you have fun,
You *slide* _____ (one).

Two
If you *jump* up when someone says boo,
Or can *stick* something together with gooey glue,
You *crawl* _____ (two).

Three
If you like to *slide* on something slippery,
And can *climb* like a chimpanzee,
You *skip* _____ (three).

Four
If you have *seen* shells at the seashore,
Or can *stomp* about like a dinosaur,
You *tip-toe* _____ (four).

Five
If you like to go in a submarine for a deep-sea dive,
Or take a sports car for a test-drive,
You *kick* _____ (five).

(cont.)

Six
If you *measure* something with yardsticks,
Hear peep, peep, peep from a brood of chicks,
You *march* _____ (six).

Seven
If you can count to eleven,
You *leap* _____ (seven).

Eight
If you *study* hard and *concentrate,*
Stop what you are doing and *hesitate,*
You *walk* _____ (eight).

Nine
If monkeys *swing* on a vine,
And people ask, "Will you be mine?"
You *stomp* _____ (nine).

Ten
If you have *read* the "Little Red Hen,"
Touched a fuzzy peach's skin,
You *stamp* _____ (ten).

End
That's all. You are done.
Yes, this game is easy and fun!

Creative Closure:

1. Can you name a movement that requires good balance?

2. Who can combine three different movements?

SHAPES AND SYMBOLS

Primary Learning Objective: The children will increase their understanding of shapes and perform movements related to specific shapes.

Materials and Equipment: Construction paper with drawings of shapes

Formation: Children are in their personal spaces.

Individual or Partner Learning Experience:
The teacher presents the following:

1. Our world is filled with shapes. All objects have some form or shape. *Point* to your body parts that are round. Can you *move* one of these round body parts?

2. People's faces can be square, round, oval, or heart-shaped. The shape of a person's mouth can make him or her look happy or sad. Show me a happy mouth, a sad mouth, and a surprised mouth.

3. People build shapes. *Make* yourself into an airplane shape, a box shape, and a bridge shape.

4. Nature produces some very large shapes. Can you be a pointed mountain?

5. Animals have shapes that help them move. Pretend you are a dolphin *moving* through the water. Is it possible to have the wings of a bird *flying* in the sky?

6. There are long narrow shapes that stand tall or lie on the ground. Is it possible to *stand* like a telephone pole? Now *lie* down like a log on the ground. *Shake* your two longest body parts.

TRIANGLE
A triangle has three sides and three corners. Each of the objects I identify have three sides and three corners
1. *Wave* a banner
2. *Cut* a pie into slices
3. *Eat* a wedge of cheese.
4. *Climb* to the top of a roof.
5. *Dig* in the garden with a trowel

SQUARE
Squares have four sides of the same length. Each of the objects I name have four sides the same length.
1. *Open* a present
2. *Stack* five blocks
3. *Fold* a handkerchief
4. *Melt* like an ice cube
5. *Toss* and *catch* a bean bag.

CIRCLE
Circles are round shapes. Each of the objects I mention have round shapes.
1. *Be round* like the letter "O"
2. *Roll* like a wheel
3. *Rise* like the sun
4. *Wind* a ball of yarn
5. *Throw* a baseball
6. *Move* like a yo-yo
7. *Bite* into a cookie
8 *Crawl* though a hoop
9. *Grip* a steering wheel
10. *Burst* like a bubble

(cont.)

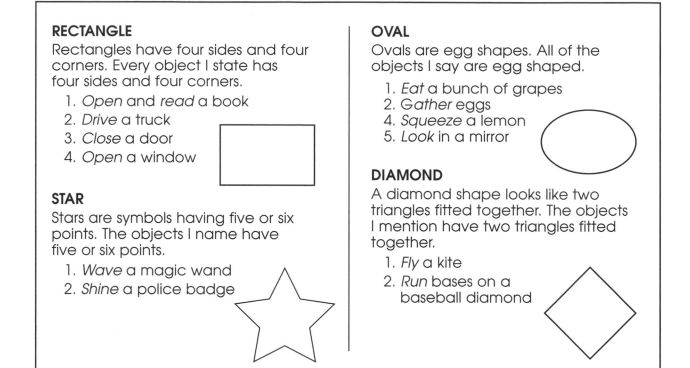

RECTANGLE

Rectangles have four sides and four corners. Every object I state has four sides and four corners.

1. *Open* and *read* a book
2. *Drive* a truck
3. *Close* a door
4. *Open* a window

STAR

Stars are symbols having five or six points. The objects I name have five or six points.

1. *Wave* a magic wand
2. *Shine* a police badge

OVAL

Ovals are egg shapes. All of the objects I say are egg shaped.

1. *Eat* a bunch of grapes
2. *Gather* eggs
4. *Squeeze* a lemon
5. *Look* in a mirror

DIAMOND

A diamond shape looks like two triangles fitted together. The objects I mention have two triangles fitted together.

1. *Fly* a kite
2. *Run* bases on a baseball diamond

Whole-Group Learning Experience:

SUPER SHAPES: Divide the children into groups of four or five. Explain to the children that you will name a specific shape. Draw the shape on construction paper for all the children to see. Encourage the children in each group to combine their bodies to create objects associated with that shape. Each group will take a turn demonstrating their object, while other groups try to name the object. For younger children, challenge each group to use their bodies to form the shape mentioned and shown.

Creative Closure:

1. Which shape had the most number of objects?

2. What shape is your favorite toy? Can you make that shape with your body?

PUZZLING SHAPES

Primary Learning Objective: The children will work collectively in a vigorous movement activity to construct a puzzle.

Materials or Equipment: Two or more duplications of a puzzle containing 25 to 40 cardboard pieces. Puzzles with fewer and larger pieces are suggested for preschool age children. Containers for each puzzle.

Formation: Children are in their personal spaces.

Individual or Partner Learning Experience:
The teacher presents the following:

1. Puzzle pieces come in different shapes and sizes. Some pieces have bumps with rounded corners. *Point* to any part of your body that has a bump (e.g., elbow, knee, heel).

2. Place your body at a low level to *create* a flat puzzle piece.

3. Can you *combine* your special puzzle shape with a classmate's shape? Try fitting the pieces together at a low level.

4. Try to make a different puzzle shape with your partner.

5. Is it possible to work with two other partners and make a four-person puzzle?

Whole-Group Learning Experience:
PUZZLE RACE: Divide the children into two to four groups of no more than three or four children, depending on the number of available puzzles. Arrange each group in a single-file line of equal distance to the puzzle pieces. On the teacher's signal, children have a turn at moving (e.g., run, skip, hop, or jump) to the containers of pieces. Each child takes one piece of his or her group's puzzle and returns to the line. Group members cooperate to complete the puzzle. After each puzzle is completed, challenge each group to create a giant group puzzle on the floor, using their bodies.

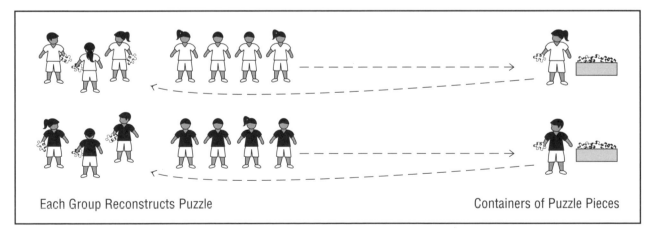

Each Group Reconstructs Puzzle   Containers of Puzzle Pieces

Creative Closure:

1. Who can name a piece of clothing that must fit snugly over our bodies (e.g., socks, gloves, hat, shoes)?

2. Show me how your fingers can act like puzzle pieces.

BODY ILLUSTRATIONS AND SHAPES

Primary Learning Objective: The child will outline the shape of a partner's body, and perform a variety of movement skills using one's own body outline.

Materials or Equipment: A box of chalk, shoe polish, or a roll of art paper with markers

Formation: Children are in their personal spaces.

Individual or Partner Learning Experience:
The teacher presents the following:

1. Different people have different body shapes. Who can show me a very tall body shape, a short body shape, a strong body shape?

2. Some people's bodies are long and narrow. Can you *make* this shape?

3. Find a way to make a round body shape.

4. Pretend your legs are rubberbands. *Stretch* your legs and make them the longest they can be.

5. We can even *make* our bodies into silly shapes. Show me a silly shape, and a strange, twisted shape.

6. Tell the children that words like "fat" and "ugly" should not be used to describe a person's body. These words make people feel sad about their body's shape.

Whole-Group Learning Experience:
BODY ILLUSTRATIONS: Organize the children into groups of four. Give each set of partners a piece of chalk. One partner lies on the floor or ground and makes a wide body shape. The partner traces around the head, arms, and legs to form the outline of the body. Partners can also trace each other's body on art paper and tape it to the floor. Partners exchange roles until both body shapes are formed.

Challenge the children to stand at the head of their body shape, on the arm, or at the feet, and to form a tunnel around their eyes with their hands looking downward over the shape. Ask the children to walk, hop, gallop, and jump around the outside of the body shape. Encourage children to run, and jump, or leap over their body shape. See if the children can jump from one hand to the other, from the feet to the head, and from one knee to an elbow.

Creative Closure:

1. Who can tell me something special about their body shape? How will your body shape change as you grow older? Show me.

2. Can you show me other movements using the outline of your body's shape (e.g., standing on one hand and one leg, jumping in and out of the shape, or standing on both knees).

TERRIFIC TRIANGLES

Primary Learning Objective: The child will recall concepts related to the triangle while participating in vigorous movement activities.

Materials or Equipment: Lively music if possible

Formation: Children are in their personal spaces.

Individual or Partner Learning Experience:
The teacher presents the following:

1. Many years ago a group of people known as the Greeks became interested in a shape called the triangle. A triangle is a shape that has three sides.

   The three sides meet at three points. The first triangle we will learn about has three sides of the same length (equilateral). Let's find several triangles that are hidden in our body. The first triangle can be made with your hands. Can you *touch* your two middle fingers together? Now *touch* your thumbs together. What shape do you see?

2. Can you *trace* a line across your face from ear to ear? Now follow down to your chin and move from the chin to the other ear. We have three points on our face that make a triangle. Find a classmate and trace the triangle shape on his or her face.

3. Show me how you can *make* a triangle shape by *bending* forward and *touching* the floor with one hand.

Whole-Group Learning Experience:
TRIANGLE TUNNELS: Divide the children into two groups. One group forms partners who grasp each other's hands. They touch the inside feet and stretch or lean backwards to make a giant triangle between them. The remaining children either move through the giant middle triangle or they may crawl under the triangle made from either of the two children's legs.

THREE TOUCHES: Review the concept of three sides. Select lively music. When the music stops, all children tap three different body parts. The music continues and the actions are repeated.

TRIANGLE JUMPS: Use masking tape or chalk to make five to seven large triangle shapes on the floor. Leave adequate space between the triangles. All children perform movement skills until a signal is given. Individual children then rush to the closest triangle and jump in and out three times. The activity continues.

Creative Closure:

1. What objects come to mind when you think of the triangle shape (e.g., roof, pennant, slice of pie)?

2. Can you trace a triangle shape on the floor using one foot without losing your balance?

THINK AND MOVE WITH WORDS

Primary Learning Objective: The children are challenged to complete a sentence with a logical answer and demonstrate the action of the sentence.

Materials or Equipment: None

Formation: Children are in their personal spaces.

Individual or Partner Learning Experience:
The teacher presents the following:

1. Invent a crazy word and move like that word.

2. Can you think of another way of moving for your word?

3. Combine your word with a partner's word for a fun way of moving.

Whole-Group Learning Experience:
THINK AND MOVE: Remind the children that the names of objects and actions are "words." Explain to the children that the following activity is an active guessing game, and that it is their role to read a sentence that has one word missing. All children are then challenged to fill in the blank and to demonstrate the action of the sentence. Use the following example:

"I can *bounce* a _____ with two hands."

In this example, the children should orally reply "ball" followed by a brief demonstration of the bouncing action.

---

1. I can *hide* under a _____ (bed, table, etc.)

2. I can *climb* a tall _____ (tree, hill, mountain, etc.)

3. I can *walk* down _____ (stairs, steps, etc.)

4. I can *open* a _____ (present, door, etc.)

5. I *sleep* in a _____ (bed, cot, etc.)

6. I *sit* on a _____ (chair, couch, etc.)

7. I *ride* in a _____ (car, bus, truck, etc.)

8. I can *stack* _____ (blocks, books, boxes, etc.)

9. I can *pull* a _____ (wagon, toy, etc.)

10. I can *leap* over a _____ (puddle, etc.)

11. I can *prance* like a _____ (horse, etc.)

---

12. I can *skate* on _____ (ice, etc.)

13. I can *march* like a _____ (robot, soldier, etc.)

14. I can *slither* like a _____ (snake, etc.)

15. I can *spin* like a _____ (helicopter, top, etc.)

16. I can *waddle* like a _____ (duck, etc.)

17. I can *wiggle* like a _____ (worm, etc.)

18. I can *burst* like a _____ (bubble, etc.)

19. I can *melt* like _____ (ice cream, snow, wax, ice, etc.)

20. I can *jump* _____ (rope, etc.)

21. I can *trudge* through the _____ (snow, mud, etc.)

22. I can *sway* like a _____ (flower, tree, etc.)

23. I can *flutter* like a _____ (butterfly, leaf, etc.)

24. I can *float* like a _____ (cloud, bubble, boat, etc.)

25. I can *sing* like a _____ (bird, sparrow, robin, parakeet, etc.)

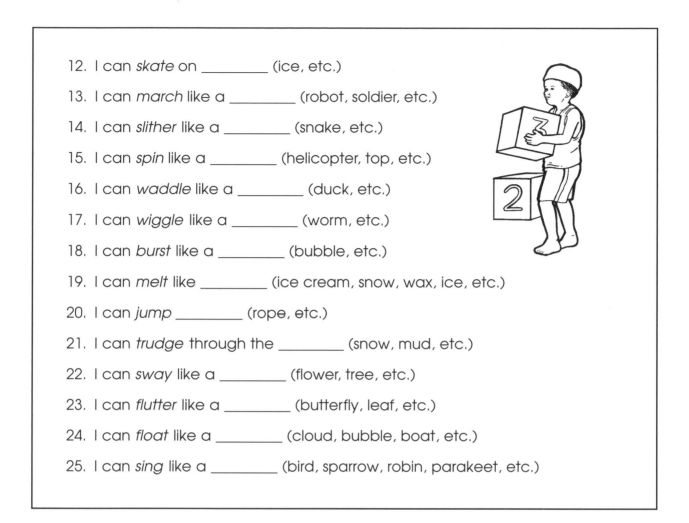

Creative Closure:

1. Who can tell the class about their most favorite guessing game?

2. Can anyone think of another action sentence with a partner and share with the group?

SPECIAL SURFACES AND SUBSTANCES

Primary Learning Objective: The children will differentiate between unique surfaces and substances while imitating movements associated with specific surfaces and substances.

Materials or Equipment: None

Formation: Children are in their personal spaces.

Individual or Partner Learning Experience:
The teacher presents the following:

1. One way that we can learn about our environment is by *exploring* as many different surfaces and substances as possible.

2. Who can describe your favorite play object? Can you describe its shape, color, and how to use it for play?

3. Is your favorite object fuzzy and soft, or hard and smooth?

4. I will say a word that describes how something feels when it is touched or used. For example:

   "I am thinking of 'fuzzy' objects or things. Show me how you hug a teddy bear."

   The child should respond by pretending to *squeeze* a stuffed fuzzy bear.

1. I AM THINKING OF **"STICKY"** OBJECTS OR THINGS.	2. I AM THINKING OF **"FUZZY"** OBJECTS OR THINGS.
a. Pretend your body is **bubble gum** being *chewed*. b. *Show* me sticky **fingers**. c. What would happen if both hands were covered with **glue** and you *touched* your ankles? d. How would you *move* if it were a hot, muggy, sticky **day**? e. Can you think of other **sticky** objects?	a. Use a **cotton ball** to *powder* your face like a clown. b. Put on your **mittens** and make-believe you are *making* a snowperson. c. *Pull* on your winter **cap** or **hat** and *roll* in the snow. d. Make-believe you are *shaking* a round, fuzzy **rug**. e. Who can think of other **fuzzy** objects or things?

3. I AM THINKING OF "SHARP" OBJECTS OR THINGS.

a. Use a make-believe **knife** to *cut* a piece of cake.

b. *Shoot* an **arrow** from a bow into a target.

c. *Thread* a **needle** and pretend to *sew* a pair of pants.

d. *Walk* as if you have a sharp **pain** in one leg.

e. Let's try to think of other **sharp** objects.

4. I AM THINKING OF "SMOOTH" OBJECTS OR THINGS.

a. *Swing* a baseball **bat** and hit a home run.

b. *Feel* the **skin** on your face and arms.

c. Pretend to *pat* a cat's **fur**.

d. Who can think of other **smooth** objects?

5. I AM THINKING OF "ROUGH" OBJECTS OR THINGS.

a. Use **sandpaper** to *polish* a wooden chair.

b. Show me how a bulldozer *pushes* **gravel** into large piles.

c. Can you use a shovel and *fill* a pail with **dirt**?

d. Make-believe you are *shaving* a **beard** from your face.

e. Can you think of other **rough** objects?

6. I AM THINKING OF "SLICK" OBJECTS OR THINGS.

a. Make-believe you are *swimming* in a brook filled with slick **rocks**.

b. How would you *walk* on a slippery **sidewalk**?

c. *Drive* a sled over the slick **ice**.

d. Show me how you *position* your body when you are moving down a **slide**.

e. Who can think of other **slick** objects?

7. I AM THINKING OF SOME VERY SPECIAL "SUBSTANCES" FOUND IN OUR NEIGHBORHOOD.

a. Show me how **Jell-O** *moves* when you eat it.

b. *Spread* **peanut butter** on two slices of bread.

c. Is it possible to *make* your body light and fluffy like **whipped cream**?

d. Make-believe you are *stirring* a large pot of **chocolate pudding**.

e. Show me how **sand** *runs* through your fingers at the beach.

f. Can you *shape* and *pat* a **mud pie**?

g. Pretend to *rub* **lotion** all over your body.

h. Show me that you can *shake* a can and *sprinkle* **powder** all over your body.

i. Let's try to think of other special **substances**.

Creative Closure:

1. Move like your favorite object discussed today.

2. Let's use our imagination to swim in a cup of hot chocolate with marshmallow floats.

MOVEMENT MORSE CODE

Primary Learning Objective: The older child will successfully substitute movements with symbols associated with the Morse Code in a whole-group learning experience.

Materials or Equipment: A large sheet of paper with the Morse Code Symbols written in large print

Formation: Children are scattered throughout the playing area.

Individual or Partner Learning Experience:
The teacher presents the following:

1. Samuel Morse invented the first successful electric telegraph. He also invented a coding system that sent messages along a wire in the form of dots, dashes, and spaces. This became known as the Morse Code. We can physically spell our names in Morse Code by performing a hop when the letter calls for a dot, and by substituting a jump when a dash occurs in the letter.

A	·▬	G	▬▬·	M	▬▬	T	▬
B	▬···	H	····	N	▬·	U	··▬
C	▬·▬·	I	··	O	▬▬▬	V	···▬
D	▬··	J	·▬▬▬	P	·▬▬·	W	·▬▬
E	·	K	▬·▬	Q	▬▬·▬	X	▬··▬
F	··▬·	L	·▬··	R	·▬·	Y	▬·▬▬
				S	···	Z	▬▬··

2. Let's practice first by spelling your name and substituting a *hop* for a dot and a *jump* for a dash. (Demonstrate the name ANN to reinforce the process.)

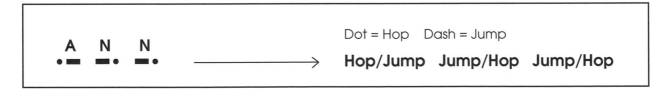

A N N
·▬ ▬· ▬· ⟶ Dot = Hop   Dash = Jump
Hop/Jump   Jump/Hop   Jump/Hop

Whole-Group Learning Experience:
MOVEMENT MORSE CODE: Challenge the group to physically spell the word "movement."

Creative Closure:

1. The dots and dashes are symbols used in the Morse Code to represent letters. Can you show me how to move like the color symbols seen in a stoplight?

2. Who can name a different favorite word to spell and move?

IMAGINATIVE NARRATIVES

Primary Learning Objective: The child will increase his or her language arts skills while imitating actions and expressive feelings of the characters in the fictional movement narratives.

Materials or Equipment: None

Formation: Children are scattered throughout the playing area.

Individual or Partner Learning Experience:
The teacher presents the following:

The selections of narratives, for each chapter, are presented in a progressive order beginning with the simplest narrative, and moving toward the more complex. Read through the narratives while noting the complexity of the movement challenges. Select a narrative that would be age- and stage-appropriate for your class and proceed from there.

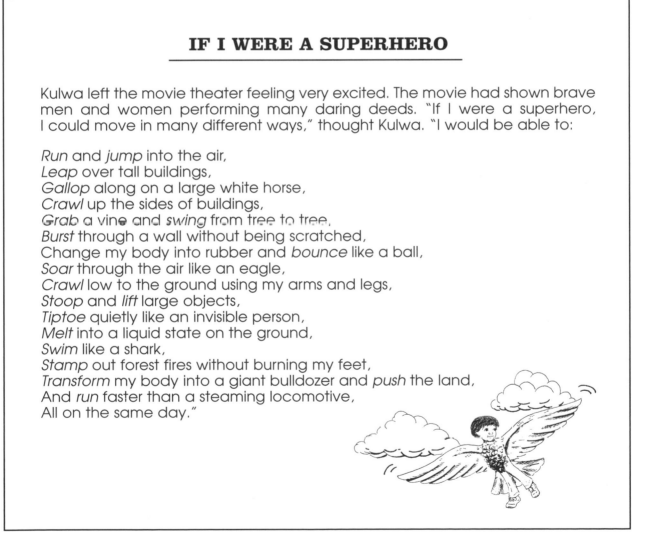

IF I WERE A SUPERHERO

Kulwa left the movie theater feeling very excited. The movie had shown brave men and women performing many daring deeds. "If I were a superhero, I could move in many different ways," thought Kulwa. "I would be able to:

Run and *jump* into the air,
Leap over tall buildings,
Gallop along on a large white horse,
Crawl up the sides of buildings,
Grab a vine and *swing* from tree to tree,
Burst through a wall without being scratched,
Change my body into rubber and *bounce* like a ball,
Soar through the air like an eagle,
Crawl low to the ground using my arms and legs,
Stoop and *lift* large objects,
Tiptoe quietly like an invisible person,
Melt into a liquid state on the ground,
Swim like a shark,
Stamp out forest fires without burning my feet,
Transform my body into a giant bulldozer and *push* the land,
And *run* faster than a steaming locomotive,
All on the same day."

WHAT WILL I GROW UP TO BE?

Saravina *stood* very still as Margareth measured her height. She was three feet and three inches tall. A *frown* came across Saravina's face as she *dropped* her chin to her chest. Her greatest dream was to be tall and strong and a very special person. "What will I grow to be?" she wondered.

Maybe one day, I'll be a baker,
Mixing bread, cookies, and cakes.
I'll *shake* and *stir* and *measure*,
Until the batter is ready to bake!

Maybe one day, I'll be an astronaut,
Flying among the stars.
I'll *zoom* by all the planets:
Pluto, Jupiter, and even Mars!

Maybe one day, I'll be a gardener.
I'll *pull* and *yank* every weed in sight.
My peas and beans will *stretch* upward,
As I watch with great delight!

Or, maybe one day, I'll be a dancer,
Twirling and *spinning* around.
Sounds of lively music will thrill me,
As I *leap* forward and *land* without a sound!

Saravina was continuing the daydream when she heard the sound of her grandmother's car. She decided, "Maybe today I'll be Saravina at three feet, three inches tall, and I'll *skip* to the door to greet my grandmother, because I can have fun being small!

BEING SMALL

Nathan watched the tiny insect *curl* its body
into a small ball shape. "Being small might be great fun,"
thought Nathan. "If I were very small, I could:

Ski down my bedroom pillow,
Sit in a peanut shell and *paddle* a canoe,
Swim in a teacup swimming pool,
Jump rope with a shoestring,

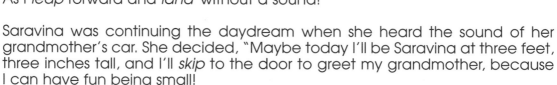

Hit a home run with a toothpick,
Drive a toy car,
Jump up and down on a kitchen sponge,
Squeeze through cracks in the wall,
Climb a hair comb ladder,
Skate on an ice cube,
Hide in a bottle cap and never be found,
Roll a marble bowling ball,
Float to the ground using a tissue paper parachute,
Touch my toes three times on a potholder exercise mat,
Fly on the back of a buzzing bee,
Or, I could *curl* into a small ball shape like the tiny insect and sleep in a slipper."

WHAT TIME "S" IT?

"What time is it, mother?" asked Scott from his bedroom door. Scott didn't wait for his mother's answer.

With a sly *grin*, Scott decided it was time to:
Stamp one foot up and down,
Stroll throughout the room,
Sink low to the floor in a flat shape,
And, *shake* my body from head to toe.

"Maybe, "thought Scott, "it's time to:
Shrink into a tiny shape,
Stretch into a long shape,
Sway my body from side to side,
And, *spin* around and around in a circle.

"Of course," thought Scott, it could be time to:
Strut around my room feeling very proud,
Slither like a snake along the floor,
Scuffle my feet as I walk, or
Swim in my bathtub."

Scott's mother decided to *sneak* upstairs and surprise Scott. "I think it is time to tidy up your room," said Scott's mother. With that suggestion, Scott gave a big *smile*, *squeezed* his toys, and knew that it was time to clean his room.

MAGICAL MOVEMENTS IN THE HOME

Rosie could not fall asleep. "I know," she said. "I'll sneak to the kitchen and prepare a snack." With that idea, she *tossed* the blankets from her body and *reached* upward for her robe. "Where are those slippers?" asked Rosie, as she *stooped* downward and *searched* under her bed.

Quietly, Rosie *tiptoed* down the stairs so as not to wake her parents. She was just about to open the refrigerator door when a very strange thing happened. The refrigerator said, "Hello, Rosie, you should be sleeping soundly in bed."

Rosie took three *jumps* backward. "You talked!" she shouted, "Refrigerators can't talk." Rosie was *shaking* with fright.

"Well, maybe some do not talk, but I do," said the refrigerator. The refrigerator told Rosie not be afraid, and asked her if she would like to join a kitchen party.

"OK," said Rosie, as she *took* her hands away from her eyes and *stood* very tall. "What do I do?" she asked.

The frying pan told Rosie to make-believe she was *breaking* two eggs and *scrambling* them with a fork. Rosie also pretended to be a long strip of bacon *sizzling* in the pan. "Show me how hot you can be," said the stove.

The toaster challenged Rosie to *stoop* down low and on the count of three *shoot* upward. One, two, three, up *jumped* Rosie for the slice of toast.

The handmixer told Rosie to use her arms and *whip* the pancake batter. "Don't forget to *flip* the pancakes before they burn," said the mixer.

"Let's see, what we should drink," said the refrigerator. The juicer asked Rosie to *squeeze* three oranges. The coffee maker asked if Rosie could *jump* up and down very quickly like the percolator brewing strong coffee.

Rosie was beginning to feel *tired*. Her head and shoulders *leaned* forward. "Rosie, oh Rosie, we can make a milk shake!" exclaimed the blender. Rosie's body *tensed* as she *sprang* upward and *saluted* the blender.

As she *walked* to the refrigerator door, Rosie *shivered* from the cold. She *stretched* and *reached* for the milk and carefully *poured* it into the blender. "*Turn* the crank on the can opener to open the chocolate syrup," instructed the blender. "Now *dig* deeply into the ice cream tub and *scoop* the large balls of ice cream." Rosie *screwed* the cover on the blender so as not to spill the milk shake.

With a *push* of one button, she began to *race* around in a circle while *waving* her arms to mix all the ingredients together. "Is it a milk shake yet?" asked Rosie.

"Yes," said the blender.

"Time to clean the kitchen," said the refrigerator. With that suggestion, the dishwasher challenged Rosie to *wave* her hands in a *splashing* motion. The vacuum cleaner asked to be *pushed* and *pulled* forward, to the side, and in a zigzag direction.

"Wait, I seem to be doing all the work for this party," said Rosie as she *collapsed* into a chair.

Rosie was *awakened* by a *tap* on her shoulder. "Wake up, sleepy head," whispered her mother. "It's time to *jump* out of bed and help me prepare a large healthy breakfast."

Rosie slowly *rolled* over and *wiped* the sleepy seeds from her eyes. "Thank you Mother, a bowl of cereal and a small glass of milk would do nicely," was all she said as she thought back on her midnight visit to the kitchen.

BEYOND THE RAINBOW

Jay *skipped* to the window. It was no longer raining. He said, "*Look*, Eileen, a giant rainbow has formed in the sky!"

"Oh hum," replied Eileen. "I have seen a rainbow before."

"Maybe you have Eileen, but this one ends in our backyard!" shouted Jay. The two children *rushed* outside. They began to *hunt* and *search* for the pot of gold that is supposed to be at the end of every rainbow. After *crawling* around the bushes, *leaping* over mud puddles, and *searching* under every rock, the two children *plunked* their bodies down. "I do not understand," said Jay. "There should be a pot of gold."

Suddenly, a tiny green man appeared. He was only six inches tall. "Perhaps, children, I can help you find a treasure of gold." The two children *jumped* up with excitement. They *watched* the little man *pick* up a stick from the ground and *point* to the grass. The grass was green. The little man said, "Show me how your body can be long and narrow like a tall blade of grass." Then he pointed to a green grasshopper and a green frog. "Can you *rub* your legs together and *jump* from flower to flower like the grasshopper? *Stoop* down on your hands and feet and use all of your muscles to *jump* like a frog."

The little green man *pointed* his stick at the colorful treasures in the fruit and vegetable garden. He said, "See if you can *make* the shape of a large orange pumpkin. Bend carefully and pull the orange carrot from the ground. Who can *stretch* up on their toes toward the blue sky to *pick* red apples? Try to be as *tiny* as the red cherries hanging from the tree. Can you *combine* your bodies to form a bunch of purple grapes?"

The little man *paused* a moment while the children *rested*. He then motioned the children to *gallop* to the oak tree. "Wonderful," thought Jay. "Maybe the gold is hidden in the tree."

The little man asked the children to *place* their hands on their heads and to *stoop* low to the ground. "Hee hee, you've made the cap and the shape of a brown acorn!" laughed the little man. The two children responded by *scurrying* along on their hands and feet pretending to be black ants. "You may *stand* now," said the little man. "It is time for me to go."

The two children just began to *stretch* their bodies into a tall shape when they both shouted, "No, wait! We did not find the gold!"

"Oh yes you did children," said the little man as he started to float away. "You found the gold when you first entered your backyard. *Stretch* upward and look in the sky."

"Oh," said the children as they *glanced* upward. The sun's golden rays shone brightly into their eyes.

THE GREAT WIZARD

A long, long time ago in a neighborhood far, far away lived a small boy named Topple. It was Topple's dream to become a fearless knight and to slay mean dragons with his sword. Everyday, Topple would *tiptoe* to the garden to watch the knights train for this job. Topple liked to *grab* a long stick and pretend it was a mighty sword. He would *charge* forward and *plunge* the sword into the air.

He knew that knights needed to be very *strong* and *quick* on their feet. He practiced *marching* in circles, *shuffling* his feet very quickly, *crouching* downward, and *hiding* behind rocks. He learned how to *spring* upward, *pointing* his stick into the air.

One day, the tallest knight spied Topple *skipping* back and forth to make his leg muscles stronger. "Would you like to join the other knights in hunting for a dragon?" the tall knight asked. Topple *jumped* up three times with excitement. He *ran* to *snatch* his stick, and with one big *leap* he *landed* on the knight's white horse.

The two riders *galloped* along on the horse, *searching* and *exploring* the deep forest. Finally, one knight began to wave a large flag. All the knights *bounded* off their horses. Topple *smacked* the ground with a big kerplunk!

Suddenly Topple began to feel very *timid* and *small*. He *coiled* his body into a tiny shape. His shoulders *shivered* with fear, "What am I doing here?" he thought.

Topple *felt* a tap on his shoulder. He *hid* his head in his hands fearing that it might be a fire-breathing dragon *stomping* through the forest. He slowly *lifted* his head. It was the Great Wizard *looking* down at him. "Topple, do you really want to slay a dragon?" asked the wizard.

"No," replied Topple. "I want to return to the castle where I am safe from dragons and swords."

"Very well," said the wizard as he *waved* a wand over Topple's head.

Topple felt his body *twirling* and *spinning* around and around until he heard a thump. He was *sitting* quietly in his mother's large wooden chair. "There's my brave boy," said Topple's mother. "What do you have in your hand, a make-believe sword?"

"Oh no," said Topple, "That could be dangerous. My stick is a make-believe wand so I can practice *flying* through the sky like the Great Wizard who rescues little boys and girls from wicked dragons."

"Very well," said Topple's mother, "But first you must *wash* your hands for dinner." "Yes," said Topple as he *tossed* the stick into the fireplace and *smiled*.

FAIRY TALE MOVEMENT

Each night, Arlene's father asked her the same question. "Which fairy tale would you like to hear this evening?"

Each night, Arlene replied by saying, "All of them Father." One evening, Arlene's father decided to grant his daughter's request. He began the task by asking her to make-believe she was a character in the fairy tale. Feeling very *fearless*, she *stretched* her body into a strong shape as her father began the story.

He said, "Once upon a time a little girl named Gretel began *searching* to find her brother Hansel. She started her journey by *galloping* down a narrow, twisted road to the shoemaker's house. "Have you seen my brother, Mr. Elf?" asked Gretel.

"No, but please help us *stretch* this leather, and *hammer* a pair of shoes," said the elves. Gretel helped *stretch* and *hammer* before *sneaking* over to see the Big Bad Wolf.

"Help me *huff* and *puff* and *blow* down this house, and we will learn if Hansel is inside," said the Wolf. Gretel *tried* three times until she *collapsed* to the ground. Hansel was not inside. "If you move quickly, Little Red Riding Hood will be *skipping* through the forest," said the wolf. Gretel *tramped* through the deep forest.

She *climbed* a large tree to locate Little Red Riding Hood. "*Come skip with me* and we might see Hansel," said Little Red Riding Hood.

After *skipping* down a dark path, Gretel decided to stop and ask Cinderella. "I'm certain Hansel will be at the ball," said Cinderella. Gretel joined Cinderella and other people on the dance floor. She *shuffled* her feet quickly for one dance, *spun* around in a circle for a second dance, and *clapped* and *kicked* up her heels on the third dance.

"This is wonderful," thought Gretel, "But it is twelve o'clock and I must leave since Hansel is not here."

Gretel was becoming very *sad*. Her body *drooped* forward when Cinderella said, "I know where Hansel might be. He must be visiting Snow White."

Gretel *trudged* up the hill to the castle door. She *tiptoed* past the wicked queen. "Maybe one of the Seven Dwarfs can help me," thought Gretel. Grumpy *stomped* both feet and was no help at all. Sleepy *curled* his body into a tiny ball and *closed* his eyes. Bashful *hid* his face while talking to Gretel, and Sneezy could not stop *sneezing*. Happy *pranced* and *strutted* along, but he had not seen Hansel.

Night began to fall. Gretel's body *was* feeling very *heavy*. She *strolled* slowly to her gingerbread home. Just then Hansel *jumped* out from behind a large rock.

"Where have you been my brother?" asked Gretel."

"First," said Hansel, "I used my strong arms to *climb* a large beanstalk with Jack. Then, I helped three bears *mix* and *stir* a large pot of porridge. Finally, I *pushed* a mean, old, wicked witch into the oven and *fastened* the bolt."

"Oh Hansel," said Gretel, "You did make my body *tremble* with worry. I'm so *glad* you had a quiet day."

"Father!" yelled Arlene, "That is a silly ending to the fairy tale."

"Yes," said Arlene's father, "I should have added that Hansel and Gretel lived happily ever after." With this ending, Arlene *placed* her hands at the side of her face and fell fast *asleep*.

THE WORLD'S GREATEST MACHINE

Marco and Rosilee were *excited* to visit the Machine Factory. They knew that each object in the factory challenged visitors to move in special ways. The trip through the factory would end when the two children found the "World's Greatest Machine."

The first learning center was called the "Wonder Wheel." Here, the children were encouraged to *make* the shape of a wheel and to *roll* forward. Some children were even able to *roll* backwards.

The Pastel Pendulum Center was fun to watch. Marco and Rosilee were asked to *sway* their bodies to one side as far as possible, and then to *sway* their bodies in the opposite direction. The next *swaying* action was slightly smaller, and then smaller, until their bodies were *still*.

The Expanding Escalator had a sign that said, "Walk to the Stars." To perform this challenge the children pretended to *walk* upstairs for one minute.

The Exercise Elevator encouraged the children to *stoop* into a small shape, and then slowly *rise* upward into a *stretched* shape. Rosilee liked the feeling of traveling upward.

The next learning center was the Wacky Windmill. In this center, the children pretended their *arms were large windmill sails* being turned by the wind. Marco said, "This is how we cool our home with fans!"

Both children were *excited* to move on to the Reacting Robots. They were certain that the robot must be the world's greatest machine. Much to their

(cont.)

surprise, the robots in the Machine Factory did not look like the robots we see on television. They looked like a box with one long arm! The guide at the center explained that real robots are made like a human's arm attached to a shoulder. The joints in the robot's arm *swivel* at the shoulder to *extend* its elbow and to *move* its wrist in different directions. "Real robots," said the guide, "are machines that do the same job again and again."

To demonstrate the robot's movements, the children were challenged to *stand* without moving their legs. One arm also remained *motionless* at the side. The other arm was used to *bend* in different directions and to pick up imaginary objects. This was the movement of a real robot. "Gee," said Marco, "I thought the robot would be the world's greatest machine, but I was wrong."

The guide at the Machine Factory said, "Now that our journey is almost completed, who would like to guess what the world's greatest machine is?"

Marco *raised* his hand and said, "It's a supersonic jet," as he quickly *zoomed* throughout the activity area.

Rosilee said, "It's a giant submarine," as she pretended to *dive* and *speed* through the water. Other children guessed the movement of a rocket *blasting* upward, a helicopter *twirling*, a giant cruise ship *moving* through the ocean, and an underground railway *following* curvy tunnels.

After each child had given an answer, the guide said, "These are wonderful machines, but the world's greatest machine is the heart inside your body. The heart muscle continually *pumps* blood around the body." She told the children that they had the power to make the machine pump faster by *running* quickly, *jumping* upward, *galloping* in a circle, *leaping* over imaginary objects, and by performing other fun movements. "You also have the ability to slow down this machine by *lying* quietly at a low level." With that suggestion, Marco and Rosilee decided to *rest* the world's greatest machine.

A VISIT FROM FOREIGN FRIENDS

Larva and Bory were feeling *adventurous* one evening. They decided that it would be fun to travel to a new and faraway place. They *climbed* the tall ladder and *squeezed* through the tiny door into their spaceship. Larva and Bory made themselves as *straight* and *narrow* as possible and *positioned* their bodies very low to the floor to prepare for the blastoff. The rocket started to *rumble* and *shake* and their adventure began!

As they began to *orbit* around a strange planet, they *tiptoed* over to the window. They were *shocked* by the shape of the large, round planet. They *pressed* their faces to the window and *looked* from side-to-side and up and down to see this amazing sight. They *steered* the spaceship toward the planet's surface. The ship *spun* around and around. After a great deal of *bouncing* up and down, the spaceship *landed* with a big final kerplunk! All was still.

Larva and Bory *strolled* down the stairs of the spaceship to *explore* this strange planet. Their legs were sore from the long trip. After *rubbing* and *shaking* their legs, they began to *gallop* and *see* the sights near their spaceship. Amazed, Larva and Bory *saw* many strange things.

They *discovered* soft furry animals with large ears and fluffy white tails that *hopped* to move forward. Larva and Bory thought it great fun to imitate the movements of these shy little creatures. They also saw several smaller green creatures that jumped to move forward. These creatures made a noise that sounded like, "Ribbit, ribbit." Larva and Bory tried to follow these creatures by *jumping* from one green landing pad to another.

As they moved on, Larva and Bory *stooped* downward to *pick* sweet smelling plants. They *held* the plants up to the part of their body used to smell. What a strange delightful odor. There was nothing like this at home!

Suddenly, there was a loud *crashing* noise. The two *ran* and *hid* and *made* a small shape to avoid the large animal. This creature walked on all fours by *shifting* its paws from side-to-side. After the large animal had *crawled* into a cave, Larva and Bory tried to copy the creature's movements. Later, Larva and Bory *galloped* and *leaped* like another animal they saw that had a hairy body with horns. Then they *flapped* their arms like the tiny-feathered creatures that had pointy noses and *flew* through the air.

The most amazing creatures they saw had metal bodies and their legs were four round disks. This metal animal *raced* along a zigzag path. The creature's eyes beamed with bright lights as it *swerved* to one side and then the other along the dirt pathway. The two inside parts of the creature *made* strange motions and sounds at each other. Larva and Bory *shuddered* with fright. They knew they would never see anything like this at home!

Larva and Bory made their long *climb* back up the ladder and *squeezed* through the tiny door into their spaceship. They *made* themselves as long and thin as possible and *positioned* their bodies at a low level to the floor to prepare for blastoff. It was time to go home. The spaceship *shook* and *rattled* as it *blasted* off into the clouds. Their faces were very *happy* because they had several stories to tell their friends about the exciting planet called Earth.

CHAPTER

Increasing the Child's Understanding
of Healthful Living

Increasing the Child's Understanding of Healthful Living

In recent years, early childhood professionals, physical educators, classroom teachers, and health professionals have worked together to ensure that preschool and elementary school age children gain knowledge of the essential elements required for healthy living. Throughout the United States, teacher education programs are focusing on content in such areas as understanding the human body systems and how they function, health and wellness, nutrition, the importance of healthy eating, and the need for daily physical activity.

When preschool through grade two children are provided with active movement experiences, and the opportunities to obtain an understanding of basic health-related concepts, they not only learn about their bodies and their physical capabilities, but they also develop an appreciation for physical activity. A love for physical activity is one of the most important gifts teachers and parents can give their children. Therefore, the overall goal in this chapter is to provide the teacher with content that can foster the child's joy for physical activity and the desire to be healthy.

To accomplish this goal, the movement-based learning experiences in this chapter have two distinguishing features. The first feature is aimed at expanding the child's awareness of different body parts, their function, and how nutrition affects the body's growth. All activities are presented through individual, partner, and whole-group learning experiences.

THE MANY PARTS OF ME

Shake hands with yourself and say hello.
How many parts of your body do you know?
Touch your head. *Tap* your toes.
Rub your stomach. *Wiggle* your nose.
Ears *hear*, eyes *see*.
Bend an elbow and a knee.
So many body parts that are a part of you.
We have only named a few!

Crouch down low to the ground
Where juicy strawberries can be found.
Now try to *move* while staying down low
Reaching, stretching, and *picking* as you go.

The second feature is that all of the movement activities are moderate to vigorous in nature. Moderate physical activity is easily maintained and is performed at an intensity in which heart rate and breathing are increased (NASPE, 2002). Vigorous physical activity is performed at an intensity in which heart rate and breathing are elevated to levels higher than those observed for moderate physical activity (NAPSE, 2002). Children might simply recognize these experiences as a fun way to strengthen their heart muscles while they are playing together. Moderate to vigorous movement-based learning experiences serve as an invaluable function in children's lives. They provide opportunities by which children can discover their physical capabilities, practice a variety of movement skills, and test their physical prowess. They also utilize a large number of muscles for continuous movements.

You *chase*... I flee

Can you *catch* me?

All around we *run*.

Exercise can be fun!

We'll *leap* tall buildings with a single bound

Landing firmly on the ground.

Super Kids can *jump* this way

Because they practice every day.

To assist the physical educator in curriculum planning, the movement-based learning experiences in this chapter coincide with the "precontrol" and "control" levels found in skill theme developmental sequences reflecting traveling, chasing, fleeing, and dodging (Graham, Holt/Hale, & Parker, 2004). Skill themes are fundamental movements that are later refined into more complex patterns in which learning experiences of greater complexity are built. The precontrol level symbolizes the stage at which a child is not able to consciously control or repeat a movement. At the control level, the action is closer to the child's desired response, with some additional effort and concentration.

Unlike games containing competitive elements that declare a winner and discourage the loser, many of these learning experiences encourage children to use their imagination and assume the role of a character or object to perform a group task. For example, to create a "Fruit Basket," teachers can challenge one half of the children to form a large circle to make the rim of the basket. Some of the remaining children make round orange, apple, or plum shapes. Encourage other children to make long thin banana shapes, and still others can make tiny, round, grape shapes.

Other activities ask children to link their movements together to accomplish a group challenge, and still others utilize a variety of expressive movements, creative pathways, fitness stretches, and creative images to stimulate group participation. The following five suggestions should assist teachers in using the content to expand the child's understanding of healthful living:

    a. Group participation is heightened when the goal of the movement-based learning experience is stated before, and reinforced during the activity. Whenever possible, teachers should also include content concerning the body (see "Fun Facts About Our Bodies" below).

    b. Emphasize the fact that we can use our bodies to perform a group function (e.g., "In this activity we will use our bodies to build a creative structure").

    c. Substitute the type of movement skill used to accomplish the task on a frequent basis, and discuss the outcome of this change in the Creative Closure.

    d. Whenever possible, utilize picture books and posters identifying body systems, human anatomy, bone structure, and food pyramids to reinforce academic concepts that are being presented in the movement experience.

    e. Most importantly, use powerful words to motivate the students, and incorporate a sense of humor and a smile to inspire the child's love for physical activity.

FUN FACTS ABOUT OUR BODIES

Our Cells

Preschool and Kindergarten:
1. Our body is made up of many tiny pieces called human cells. Human cells come in all shapes and sizes because of the variety of jobs they must do.
2. Some cells are round, others are flat like discs, and some look like rods. All cells are too small to be seen by the human eye.
3. Our body has many types of cells, including skin cells, bone cells, brain cells, and blood cells.

Grades One and Two:
1. Every second, millions of cells die. We are born with a surplus of brain cells to make up for this continual loss.
2. Each cell is like a city in its structure and function. It produces the energy for the body.
3. The center of the cell (i.e., the nucleus) is where the cell's information is stored.
4. The outer membrane of a cell is like a city wall, protecting the cell from harmful substances.

Our Muscles

Preschool and Kindergarten:
1. Muscles move our body, like strings move a puppet.
2. Muscles are made out of many stretchy, elastic materials called fibers.
3. We have more than 600 muscles in our body.
4. In order for a muscle to work, it must have a "partner muscle." One muscle pulls a bone forward, and another muscle pulls a bone back. When one muscle is working (i.e., contracting), the other muscle is relaxing. Muscle pairs work very well together.

5. Muscles also help hold organs in place.
6. We have a large muscle in our chest (i.e., the diaphragm) that helps our lungs breathe.
7. Our heart is also a muscle and it makes blood move through the body.
8. Muscles help us to chew our food, and even close our eyelids.
9. Muscles even help us smile, and it takes more muscles to frown than it does to smile.
10. We can learn more about the importance of our muscles by participating in the following action rhyme:

My Muscles Move Me

Muscles help your body move.
When you *stretch* them, they improve.
Your muscles are always busy at work.
They can *move quickly, slowly,* or with a *jerk.*
Use your muscles to *move your eyes,*
Then your *arms, knees, shoulders, fingers, feet,* and *thighs.*
Muscles help you do everything.
They help you to *jump forward,* and let your *arms swing.*
Move forward, backward, and to the *side.*
Move them so you are *tall and thin,* then *round, now wide.*
Make yourself as *small* as a mouse,
Then *stretch* your body as *large* as a house.

Grades One and Two:
1. Muscles are made of fibrous tissues bound together, and they act like bunches of rubber bands.
2. Muscles can only work in one way, by pulling. They never work by pushing.
3. The muscle system in our body is arranged so that even if we are pushing against something with all our strength our muscles are really pulling.
4. The ends of our muscles are attached to bones. One end is attached to a bone that the muscle is intended to move. The other end is anchored to a bone that the muscles will not move.
5. Our muscles are usually attached to the bone by a short, tough cord called a tendon.
6. Muscles are heavy. Our muscles make up half the weight of our body.
7. There are over three times as many muscles in the adult body as there are bones.
8. We use 17 muscles to smile and 43 muscles when we frown.
9. We use 72 muscles every time we speak one word.
10. Muscles become stronger when they are used.

Our Heart

Preschool and Kindergarten:
1. Our heart is a strong pump that moves blood through the body.
2. Our heart hangs slightly left in the center of our chest, and it is about the size of a person's fist.
3. The heart muscle works all the time, even when we sleep.
4. It pumps blood, which is full of a gas called oxygen, and food through tubes called arteries. The blood travels throughout our body and feeds our tiny cells.
5. Our heart pumps our blood to our lungs.
6. It takes about one minute for our heart to circle the blood around the body and back again (i.e., circulation).
7. We can hear our heart beating all the time. The beating sound is caused by the opening and closing of the doors (i.e., valves) inside the heart. They let the blood in and out of the heart.
8. When we feel our heart beating, we know that blood is circling all around the body.

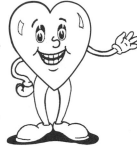

Grades One and Two:
1. Our heart is a pump that moves blood through the body. The blood is carried away from the heart in elastic tubes called arteries, and it returns to the heart in elastic tubes called veins.
2. Together the heart, blood, arteries, and veins form what is known as the circulatory system.
3. Blood carries oxygen and other important materials to every part of the body through tiny tubes called capillary arteries.
4. The heart is really two pumps. One pump gets blood from the body and sends it out to the lungs. The other pump gets blood from the lungs and sends it around the body.
5. Our heart is divided into four compartments (i.e., chambers).
6. Every contraction and relaxation of the heart produces one heartbeat.
7. A rabbit's heart is about the size of a ping-pong or golf ball.
8. Large dogs have hearts the size of tennis balls, and a giraffe has a heart the size of a basketball.
9. The heart's job is to pump blood. When blood enters the heart, the heart stretches. Then it squeezes together to push the blood out.

Our Bones

Preschool and Kindergarten:
1. Our bones give our bodies shape and support and protect our organs.
2. Bones help us to move from place to place.
3. Our bones grow longer, and we get taller.
4. Bones are strong, but they can break and mend.
5. Half of the 206 bones in our body are in our hands and feet.

Grades One and Two:
1. The frame of the bones in our body is called the skeleton.
2. The skeleton serves several purposes: the bones give the body its general support, they support and protect the softer parts of the body, and they provide leverage for the muscles that are attached to them.
3. Inside the hard, outer material of our bones is a soft yellowish substance called marrow.

4. The marrow in our bones contains many of the important materials that we need in order to live.
5. The point at which bones meet is called a joint.
6. The biggest, longest, and strongest bone in our body is the thigh bone (i.e., femur).
7. The part of the skull that encloses the brain is made up of bones with immovable joints (i.e., cranium).
8. At the joints where there is movement, the bones are bound together by strong bands called ligaments.
9. Most people have 24 ribs that form a cage that protects their heart and lungs.
10. Bones are made of living cells.

Taste and Nutrition

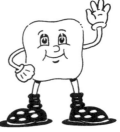

Preschool and Kindergarten:
1. Our tongue is our most sensitive body part. Our heel is the least sensitive part of our body.
2. When we eat healthy foods, the food tastes sweet, bitter, sour, or salty.
3. The way food tastes is determined when food touches our taste buds on the upper surface of the tongue.
5. Not all of our taste buds are on the tongue. There are some on the palate and some at the top of the throat on the pharynx and tonsils.
6. The taste buds at the tip of our tongue detect sweetness.
7. The taste buds at the sides of our tongue detect sourness and saltiness.
8. The taste buds near the base of our tongue detect bitterness.
9. Healthy foods come in a variety of tastes.
10. The stomach is like a stretchy storage bag that can hold up to two quarts of food. When you are hungry, your stomach muscles contract. If there is air in your stomach, this contraction will make a growling or rumbling sound.

Grades One and Two:
1. The process of breaking down food is called digestion. Our food travels throughout the body, and on its way it is broken into smaller pieces.
2. Our teeth are used to bite, chew, and chop the food into tiny pieces. The tongue also helps to make the food smaller and softer.
3. When we swallow food, it travels down our throat and through a long tube into our stomach.
4. Our stomach stretches with the food, and acids help to break it down further.
5. When food leaves the stomach, it travels down into the intestines where the nutrients of the food go into our bloodstream.
6. The food we eat must enter the bloodstream and go to the cells in our body.
7. If we think of our body as a city, then the circulatory system would be the train that travels through it. The heart sends the blood with the good nutrients on hundreds of round trips every day, each trip taking less than a minute. Every time the heart beats, it is sending another wave of blood through the body.
8. Our food consists of elements called proteins, fats, carbohydrates, vitamins, and water. We need some of all of these to live. A balanced diet contains grains (e.g., bread, cereal, rice, pasta); fruit that is fresh, dried, or unsweetened; vegetables that are raw or lightly cooked; foods high in protein (e.g., red meat, poultry, fish, dried beans, eggs, nuts); and dairy (e.g., milk, yogurt, cheese).
9. During our lifetime, we eat about 60,000 pounds of food, about the combined weight of six elephants.
10. Food is measured according to the amount of energy it produces. The unit to measure this energy is the calorie.

Our Lungs

Preschool and Kindergarten:
1. Our lungs help the body breathe.
2. The upper part of our chest is almost totally filled with lungs.
3. Our lungs are made up of millions of little sacs that fill up and let out air.
4. Our lungs can hold about as much air as a basketball.

Grades Ones and Two:
1. Air comes into our body through the nose and mouth. It travels down the wind-pipe (i.e., trachea) through tubes (i.e., bronchial tubes), and then to both lungs.
2. Our lungs trade air with the blood. The heart pumps used blood to the lungs. The lungs take the carbon dioxide and other things we can't use out of the blood.
3. Our lungs give back fresh oxygen to the blood. In a short while, the blood goes back to the heart to work again.
4. The strong muscle that helps make our lungs work is called the diaphragm.
5. The diaphragm is under the lungs. It helps push out the lungs when they are filling up with air.
6. The diaphragm also helps let our lungs back in to squeeze out the used air.
7. When we take a large breath (i.e., inhaling) or when we breathe air out (i.e., exhaling), we know the lungs are working.
8. We breathe faster after running or being physically active. This is due to the need for additional oxygen for the body.
9. Our lungs are like balloons filling up with air and letting air out.
10. People can keep their lungs healthy by moving quickly, exercising, and not smoking.

Our Brain

Grades One and Two
1. The right side of the brain receives messages, and controls the left side of our body.
2. Our brain does not move, but it uses more oxygen than any other part of our body.
3. Our brain does not grow after we are six years old.
4. The brain is our body's very special computer. It is constantly receiving information from inside and outside the body, and either uses it, or saves the information for future use.
5. Our brain uses as much energy as a 10-watt electric bulb.
6. Our brain looks like a mushroom of gray and white tissue, and it feels like jelly!
7. Our brain is about 80 percent water.
8. Our brain works best when we have a long night's sleep, and our body is in good health.

9. People say that we do not use all of our brain's capacity, but learning helps us to exercise our brain.
10. Playing outside is one way to get fresh oxygen to the brain.

FRUIT SALAD

Primary Learning Objective: The child will manipulate different body parts to keep a balloon afloat and depend on others to create an imaginary fruit salad.

Materials or Equipment: Multicolored balloons, enough for each child

Formation: Children are in their personal spaces.

Individual or Partner Learning Experience:
The teacher asks the following:

1. Who would like to select their favorite color balloon? Can each of you think of a favorite fruit that is the color of your balloon?

2. *Toss* your fruit into the air. Let it fall and touch your arm. Try again this time by *bouncing* it off your elbow. Now bounce your fruit off your knee.

3. See if you can *toss* your fruit at different heights. *Catch* your fruit over your head, in the middle of your body, near the floor/ground.

4. Can you think of a favorite game involving your fruit that you can play by yourself (e.g., Keep it Up)? Let's play "Keep it Up" using different body parts.

5. Is it possible to play "Keep it Up" while *holding* a partner's hand?

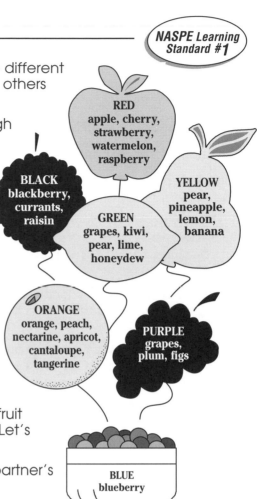

Whole-Group Learning Experience:
FRUIT CUP: Ask the children to select a partner and share one balloon. At the teacher's signal, partners explore different methods of moving the balloons between the two players (e.g., tapping, kicking, or bouncing), and different ways that the two players can move the piece of fruit to the opposite end of the playing area (e.g., holding both hands and keeping the balloon in the air, using only lower body parts to advance the balloon, using only one hand and one leg, using only the head).

FRUIT SALAD: Organize the children in groups of five. Four players form a circle and clasp hands. The fifth child asks the group what fruit they would like to have in their fruit salad, and responds to their suggestion by tossing in that colored balloon into the center of the circle.

Depending on the group's skill ability, the tosser may add a second balloon, challenging the children to keep two fruits in the air, or he or she may wait for the group to lose control of the balloon so that it drops to the floor and then add the group's second favorite fruit. This continues until the children have tossed several fruits to create an imaginary fruit salad.

Creative Closure:

1. Which body parts were the easiest to use in advancing the balloon forward?

2. Who can tell me why it is important to eat fruits every day?
   (Fresh fruits are high in vitamins.)

FUN FRUIT & VEGETABLE CHALLENGES

Primary Learning Objective: The child will find enjoyment by participating in a variety of creative stretches and will show appreciation for healthy fruits.

Materials or Equipment: None

Formation: Children are in their personal spaces.

Individual or Partner Learning Experience:
The teacher presents the following:

1. A tomato is actually a fruit that we use as a vegetable. Show me how you can *stand* and *bend* forward to touch your toes to perform a "tomatoe" (tomato) stretch.

2. Pineapples are juicy fruits that look like large pine cones. Let's *stretch* our back and perform the "spine-apple" stretch by *bending* forward with both arms and letting them dangle near the floor, and now *swinging* our arms up over our head behind our back.

3. Green beans are high in protein and carbohydrates. Can you demonstrate the string bean stretch by *clasping* your hands over your head and *stretching* to one side and then to the other side?

4. Peaches have fuzzy skin. Is it possible to *curl* your body into a round peach shape?

5. Strawberries are very high in Vitamin C. Find a way to *stretch* your body in three different directions to perform a strawberry stretch.

6. It was the Native Americans who showed the pioneers how to pop corn. Find a partner, *hold* hands, and *jump* together like popping corn.

7. Spinach contains Vitamin A. See if you can *stretch* at the waist to perform the spinning spinach. Use your elbows to start the spinning motion.

Whole Group Learning Experience:
WATERMELON WIGGLE: Organize the children into groups of four or five and encourage each group to use its imaginations and create an exercise or dance called the "Watermelon Wiggle," "Turnip Twist," "Squishy Squash," and/or "Crazy Cucumber."

Creative Closure:

1. Which body parts did we stretch today?

2. Stand and show me your favorite exercise. Raise your hand if you think you can perform this exercise three times every evening at home.

FRUIT ORIGINS: Figs (Middle East, 4500 B.C., the most frequently discussed fruit in religious writing), Grapes (Caspian and Black Sea, 4000 B.C.), Cantaloupes (Iran, 2400 B.C.), Watermelons (Central Africa, 2000 B.C.), Mandarin Oranges (China, 220 B.C.), Lemons (Burma, 11th Century), Papayas (West Indies, 14th Century), Mangoes (Southeast Asia, 16th Century), and Limes (Americas, 17th Century).

Roberts, J. (2001).

CRISPY VEGETABLES

Primary Learning Objective: While participating in a whole-group activity, the children will increase their understanding of the textures, colors, and shapes common to different vegetables

Materials or Equipment: None

Formation: Children are in their personal spaces.

Individual or Partner Learning Experience:
The teacher presents the following:

1. Raise your hand if you have ever tasted stir-fried vegetables. We know that raw vegetables that snap and crunch are cut or chopped into tiny bite-size shapes that allow them to cook faster. Fewer vitamins escape when vegetables are cooked quickly. Can you use your arms and hands to show me a *chopping* movement?

2. Pretend your body is a long narrow stalk of celery. Make-believe that your body is a *round* tearful onion.

3. Who can use his or her body to *create* a thin pointed carrot? A tiny green pea? A thin cabbage leaf? Show me how you can *create* a mushroom cap by placing your hands on your head.

4. Mixed Vegetables: Who can select a partner and form as many different types of vegetables as possible using your bodies and imaginations (e.g., peas and carrots)?

Whole-Group Learning Experience:
FRYING PAN: Ask the children to make-believe that some space of the playing area is a large frying pan. Ask them to imagine that their bodies are one of the vegetables that they made in their personal space. Encourage everyone to jump into the giant frying pan, as the teacher begins to stir the vegetables. Tell the children that as the frying pan begins to heat, they need to lift their feet off the floor.

At some point, tell the children that the heat is being turned down. They can move more slowly. Finally, turn the heat off, and the children are ready to be "eaten!" On this cue, make a gesture with your arms opening or closing, or chase the children so they all flee.

Creative Closure:

1. Who can tell me why it is important to eat fresh vegetables?

2. Can you think of any other vegetables that taste good uncooked (e.g., spinach, broccoli, cauliflower)? Use your body to create that shape.

TWISTED PRETZELS

Primary Learning Objective: The child will explore a variety of twisted shapes by rotating specific body parts.

Materials or Equipment: None

Formation: Children are in their personal spaces.

Individual or Partner Learning Experience:
The teacher asks the following:

1. Who can pretend to *open* a jar of peanuts?

2. What body part were you *twisting* in this movement? Show me.

3. Can you *twist* the upper part of your body without moving the lower part of your body?

4. Is it possible to *twist* one upper body part around a lower body part?

5. Quickly find a partner, and use as many body parts as possible to make twisted pretzel shapes.

Whole-Group Learning Experience:
TWISTED PRETZELS: Divide the children into groups of five to six. Encourage children to make a giant pretzel shape by connecting with their classmates' shapes. Each group should maintain the pretzel shape until the teacher says, "Twisted Pretzels."

Creative Closure:

1. Which body parts were the easiest to twist (e.g., shoulders, neck, hips, or wrists)?

2. What other objects have twisted pretzel-like shapes (e.g., gift bows, shoelaces, balloon animals, bow ties)? Can you make these shapes?

HEARTY SANDWICHES

Primary Learning Objective: The child will exhibit the cooperation needed to partially support his or her group member's weight and appreciate healthy foods.

Materials or Equipment: None

Formation: Children are in their personal spaces.

Individual or Partner Learning Experience:
The teacher presents the following:

1. *Raise* your hand if you know how much your body weighs.
2. What two body parts support our weight when we are standing? *Move* those body parts.
3. Can you use both legs and both hands to support your weight?
4. Is it possible to use your knees and one hand to support your weight?
5. Select three different body parts to support your weight.

Whole-Group Learning Experience:
HEARTY SANDWICH: To create a friendly atmosphere, take one child's hand and place it horizontally between your two hands. Ask the children to guess the name of the object that you have created. After several attempts, tell the children that you have made a "hand sandwich." Introduce the idea that the children can use their bodies to create a healthy sandwich. Divide the class into groups of six to eight children. Ask the groups to identify different foods and shapes that make up a sandwich (e.g., round olives, flat slices of cheese, turkey, and long pickle strips).

Begin by asking four children from each group to form the outside crust of a slice of bread while lying in a prone position (i.e., while facing downward). Two to three children are selected to be food items and carefully lie inside the crust (e.g., first the lettuce, then the tomatoes, followed by the peppers, one slice of cheese, one pickle). Complete the top slice of bread by having one child stand and form an arch shape over their group members' bodies. The activity is complete when the teacher circulates to the different sandwiches and pretends to take a large bite (i.e., by opening and closing his or her arms) of each sandwich.

Creative Closure:

1. Who can name other healthy foods to create sandwiches?
2. Which body parts were used the most to support your classmates' weight? Shake those body parts.

FANCY FINGERS & TERRIFIC TOES

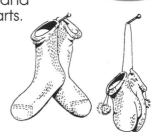

NASPE Learning Standard #2

Primary Learning Objective: The child will suggest movements and develop actions that can be performed with specific body parts.

Materials or Equipment: None

Formation: Children are in their personal spaces.

Individual or Partner Learning Experience:
The teacher presents the following:

1. Today we will explore different movements that our bodies can perform. What body parts do we cover with mittens (hands, fingers, palms, wrists)? Let's explore several hand movements. Who can *wiggle* their fingers, or flutter their fingers?

2. Follow me as I make a *clapping* motion. Now cup your hands and clap. Do you hear a different sound?

3. Make two fists and *pound* one fist on top of the other.

4. Show me how you can *drum* your fingers on the floor. *Snap* your fingers together. *Shake* your fingers at the side of the body.

5. Find other ways to move your fingers and hands (e.g., *point, push, pull, grip, dig, scoop, flick, cross, throw, catch*).

Whole-Group Learning Experience:
FANCY FINGERS AND TERRIFIC TOES: Divide the children into groups of four or five. Ask the children to identify the part of the body that we cover with socks (i.e., feet, toes, heels, ankles). Give each group three to five minutes to explore movements or gestures that can be performed with their toes and feet (e.g., wiggling, stomping, kicking, marching, and other vigorous movements). Bring the children together and have each group demonstrate two to three actions, as the remainder of the class mimics their movements.

Creative Closure:

1. Which actions today involved stretching the fingers and toes?

2. Which actions involved curling or bending these body parts?

TEN HANDS HIGH

Primary Learning Objective: The children will make comparisons between a horse's body parts and movements, and their own body parts and movements.

Materials or Equipment: None

Formation: Children are in their personal spaces.

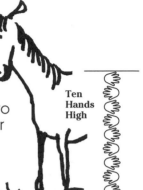

Individual or Partner Learning Experience:
The teacher presents the following:

1. Horses have two oval eyes set on the sides of their head. *Point* to where your eyes are located (i.e., in the front of the face, under the eyebrows, above the cheeks).

2. Horses have feet, called hoofs. They have one toe inside each hoof; therefore, they always walk on their tiptoes. Can you *move* throughout the playing area on your tiptoes?

3. Horses need to be brushed to remove dirt from their bodies. Use your fingers and make-believe you have a hair brush. *Brush* your fingers through your hair.

4. Horses walk forward by first stepping with their right foot, followed by a step with their left foot, then another step forward with their left foot, and one more step using their right foot. See if you can try this movement several times.

5. Prancing is a form of movement that horses perform by lifting each front leg upward as they walk. Is it possible to *lift* your knees high while you *move* around a make-believe circus ring?

6. Trotting is very similar to a person's jogging movement. Show me how you can *jog* in a large circle.

7. Who can form a rocking horse with a partner? One partner should stand and rock his or her body forward and backward while the second partner stands behind the first and gently places his or her hands on the shoulder of the first partner.

8. The height of a horse is measured from the ground to the highest point of a horse's shoulder. People who own horses use the width of one hand to determine the horse's height. Find a partner and, using your hands, take turns measuring each other's height from the floor to the shoulders.

Whole-Group Learning Experience:
HORSE AND CARRIAGE: Communicate the idea that the Morgan horse, being strong, fast, and enduring, is known for its ability to pull carriages. Ask the children to quickly form groups of three. Two of the children stand side-by-side and clasp hands. These two children are the Morgan horses. The third child stands behind the two horses and reaches forward to clasp their outside hands. This child is the carriage. All three children move forward throughout the playing area without colliding into the other carriages.

Creative Closure

1. Who can name other animals that are taller than you? Can you show me how they move?

2. What other ways can horses move (e.g., gallop, prance, jump, trot)? Show me how you can gallop with a friend.

A PILE OF BONES

Primary Learning Objective: The child will isolate and name different body parts and body areas to serve as specified targets in a vigorous movement activity.

Materials or Equipment: None

Formation: Children are in their personal spaces.

Individual or Partner Learning Experience:
The teacher presents the following:

1. Let's divide our bodies into different areas or zones.

2. Can you make three upper body parts *move* one after the other?

3. *Move* two body parts on the right side of your body. Make one of those body parts the highest part of your body.

4. *Point* to two lower body parts. See if you can make those two lower body parts *move* at the same time.

5. *Wiggle* one body part that is on the left side of the body.

Whole-Group Learning Experience:
A PILE OF BONES: Ask the children to designate a specific body part or body area to serve as a target (e.g., the elbow, the shoulder below the knees, the hip, between the shoulder blades, or the ankle). Select two or more chasers, depending on the size of the group. Challenge the remainder of the children to scatter and flee from the chaser(s). When an individual is tagged, he or she collapses into a "pile of bones." After everyone is tagged, select new chasers, or call out "Strong bodies!" Those children who are tagged continue in the game.

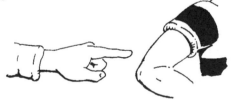

Creative Closure:

1. Which body part was the most difficult to tag?

2. Show me the movements you used to protect your body from being tagged (e.g., dodging and darting).

BODY TALK

Primary Learning Objective: The child will utilize different body parts and gestures to communicate through movement.

Materials or Equipment: None

Formation: Children are in their personal spaces.

Individual or Partner Learning Experience:
The teacher presents the following:

1. We can use our body parts to tell people things, or to communicate how we are feeling, without saying a word. Show me how you use your hands to say hello (e.g., *wave*, *shake* hands).

2. *Wave* both arms high into the air to get a friend's attention.

3. Can your shoulders show that you feel tired?

4. What movement do you use when your stomach is filled with healthy foods?

5. Make-believe that you are very strong.

6. Use your hands to say good job (e.g., thumbs up, clap).

7. How do we use our hands to tell a friend to follow?

8. Find a way to show me that your legs are very stiff, floppy, or happy and active!

Whole-Group Learning Experience:
BODY TALK: Ask the children to quickly select a "silent partner." Challenge the partners to use body gestures and movements to "talk" or communicate with each other while performing specific tasks.

Use the following two examples:

(a) The first student stoops in a small shape and indicates by a wave of the hand that the second student is to move over his or her body, and

(b) The second student motions for the first student to follow and skip to a particular side of the room by pointing to the space.

Play lively music and encourage all children to move to the way the music makes them feel.

Creative Closure:

1. Which body parts do we most often use to communicate? Show me.

2. Can anyone tell me what sign language is and who uses it?

LOOSE AND FLOPPY

Primary Learning Objective: The child will work individually and interact with a partner to relax different parts of the body.

Materials or Equipment: None

Formation: Children are in their personal spaces.

Individual or Partner Learning Experience:
The teacher presents the following:

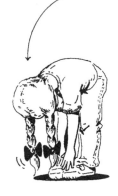

1. We live in a very busy world, and sometimes problems cause our bodies to feel very tight and troubled. Let's learn how to relax our bodies by making our arms loose and floppy.

2. Show me how you can *make* your legs loose and floppy.

3. On my signal, *stretch* all of your muscles by reaching high into the air, and then *make* them floppy. Ready, go.

4. Can you *make* floppy movements at a medium level, a high level?

5. While sitting, make your body floppy at the waist. Make your ankles loose and floppy. *Lie* down and *make* your whole body floppy and relaxed.

Whole-Group Learning Experience:
LOOSE AND FLOPPY: Explain that the children are to walk throughout the playing area until you say, "Loose and Floppy." On that signal, individual children are to move to the person standing closest to them. Partners make contact with two body parts and move them in a loose and floppy manner. Separate from the partner and walk in opposite directions until the signal is heard again. Select a different partner. Repeat the action several times.

Creative Closure:

1. Which body parts are the easiest to make loose and floppy?

2. Show me how to relax your shoulders by lifting them upward toward the chin. Now relax.

TWIST AND TWIRL

Primary Learning Objective: The child will differentiate between twisting and twirling movements while performing individual and group movement tasks.

Materials or Equipment: Four to six bean bags, floor spots, or similar small objects.

Formation: Children are in their personal spaces.

Individual or Partner Learning Experience:
The teacher asks the following:

1. How many different body parts can you *twist* (e.g., ankles, wrists, and hips)? Show me.

2. Can you show me how you can *twist* your whole body into a new shape?

3. See if you can *twist* your hips to dance back and forth.

4. Find a way to *twirl* your body around and around without losing your balance. Try again, only this time begin with your arms close to your chest, and then slowly *twirl* around while extending your arms outward.

5. Is it possible to *twirl* your body around several times and stop in a *twisted* narrow shape?

Whole-Group Learning Experience:
TWIST AND TWIRL: Ask the children to select partners. Challenge the partners to grasp hands or wrists and to twirl each other safely in a circular shape. Combine partners into groups of four. Challenge the groups to grasp hands or wrists and to twirl in a circular shape. Encourage the groups to change from a medium level to a low level while slowly raising their hands to a high level. Challenge the groups to twirl and move forward like a flying saucer.

LANDING PADS: Scatter several small objects throughout the activity area. Challenge groups of four to twirl while moving to each marker. The groups should hover over a marker for three seconds before moving on to a second marker.

Creative Closure:

1. What body parts can be easily twisted without injuring the body (e.g., ankles, wrists, and hips)? Twist those body parts.

2. What body parts did you use most to keep your balance when you were twirling in a group circle?

MAKE A MUSCLE

Primary Learning Objective: The child will experience and explain the difference between a tightened muscle and a relaxed muscle.

Materials or Equipment: None

Formation: Children are in their personal spaces.

Individual or Partner Learning Experience:
The teacher presents the following:

1. Muscles make it possible for the body to move. Our brain sends a message to a muscle or a group of muscles and tells them to tighten (i.e., contract) or to relax. To test this, we can tell our brain to *make* a tight grip or a fist. If you want to open your hand, tell your brain to relax your muscles.

2. Show me how you can *make* a strong shape with your arms. Feel your muscle grow and tighten. Now *shake* your arms to relax the muscle liked cooked spaghetti.

3. Can you *stiffen* your legs and tighten the muscles? Now *bend* your legs to a low level. This movement also tightens your muscles. *Walk* about and relax your leg muscles.

4. Who can show me an object or a person that walks with stiff legs (e.g., robot or a soldier)?

5. Is it possible to *tighten* your stomach muscles? Show me.

6. Let's lie down at a low level and *tighten* one arm muscle. Now, *relax* your arm. *Tighten* the other arm muscle. *Relax.* Try to *tighten* one leg muscle, *relax*, and then *tighten* the other leg muscle.

7. Select a partner, and extend one hand to each other in a handshake or gripped position, making your arms tight by gripping firmly. Switch hands.

8. With your partner, can you sit down facing each other with toes touching? Who can make their legs tight? Now relax.

Whole-Group Learning Experience:
Read the following muscle challenges and ask the children to demonstrate these actions.

There are so many healthy ways to have fun.
Sprinting while using our hamstrings is a special one.

Imagine you are *climbing* way up high,
On a giant, rocky mountain that rises to the sky.

Moving like a seesaw at a low level with a friend,
Becoming more fit as your muscles *stretch* and *bend*.

If becoming healthy is your aim,
Then *running* in place could be your game.

Our quadriceps help us to *jump*.
Back and forth our legs and arms *pump*.

Let's complete our muscle challenges, so *wiggle* and *shake* with all your might
To keep your muscles from becoming tight.

Creative Closure:

1. How did you feel when you relaxed your muscles?

2. See how many different ways you can stretch your upper body parts.

MOLD AND SHAPE

Primary Learning Objective: The child will mold his or her partner's body into identifiable shapes and poses, and contribute to a whole-group statue.

Material or Equipment: None

Formation: Children are in their personal spaces.

Individual or Partner Learning Experience:
The teacher asks the following:

1. Can you *tighten* your muscles and stand very still like a statue?

2. When I *clap* my hands, show me a different type of statue.

3. Who can *show* me what a silly statue might look like?

4. See if you can *change* the height of your silly statue.

Whole-Group Learning Experience:
MOLD AND SHAPE: Ask the children to explain how Play-Doh is used to make different shapes and objects (e.g., bending, stretching, rolling). Cookie dough or clay can be substituted if the children are not familiar with the Play-Doh substance. Encourage the children to move quickly and select a partner. Suggest that one child pretend to be a large can of Play-Doh. The other partner pretends to be an artist and "molds" the dough into familiar shapes (e.g., round, triangle, box, wide, long) or objects (e.g., tree, table, chair, rocket). Exchange roles.

For a greater challenge, divide the children into groups of five or six. Ask for two children to volunteer to mold their group members into larger shapes or objects to create an imaginary art gallery. All groups should demonstrate their creations to the class.

Creative Closure:

1. What kinds of shapes did we make today (e.g., narrow, tall, short, wide)?

2. Which body parts were the easiest to bend into different poses? Who can show me their favorite statue?

CREATE-A-BODY

Primary Learning Objective: The child will perform a variety of expressive movements, and work in a group to collectively illustrate the key parts of a person's body.

Materials or Equipment: Four to six large sheets of plain paper and one box of markers or crayons

Formation: Children are in their personal spaces.

Individual or Partner Learning Experience:
The teacher presents the following:

1. The look or expression on people's faces often show us how they are feeling. How does your face tell me you are feeling very worried, daring, bashful, and angry?

2. Use your whole body to tell me that you are feeling very mighty, beautiful, afraid, and sleepy.

3. How does your body *move* when you are feeling droopy, fierce, and lazy?

4. Some people skip and dance when they are feeling playful. Can you *skip* and *dance* and *move* in a playful way?

5. Show me how your favorite action heroes and heroines feel and *move*.

Whole-Group Learning Experience:
CREATE-A-BODY: Arrange the children into four to six groups of no more than three or four children, depending on the size of the class. Each group forms a single-file line with all group members facing the same direction. A large sheet of paper and a box of crayons are placed at the opposite end of each group's playing area.

Explain that the purpose of this activity is to work with other classmates in each group to draw a person's body. To do so, the first child from each line runs to their designated sheet of paper and draws a large round circle. This circle represents a person's face. After completing the circle, the child returns to the rear of his or her line. The second child in line runs to the sheet of paper and draws one eye, followed by the third child who draws a second eye. The fourth child adds a nose; the fifth draws an ear, and so on until the face is complete with eyelashes, a chin, lips, teeth, cheeks, and hair, followed by larger body segments (a neck, torso, arms, hands, fingers, legs, and feet). Vary the form of locomotor movement used to advance to the sheet of paper.

Creative Closure:

1. Who can tell me what the person they have drawn is feeling, based on the completed drawing (e.g., surprised, silly, frightened)?

2. Can your body move in other ways to show how you are feeling?

NO "BODY" IS LAST

Primary Learning Objective: The child will move consecutively from back to front while negotiating space.

Materials or Equipment: None

Formation: Partners are scattered throughout the playing area.

Individual or Partner Learning Experience:
The teacher presents the following:

1. Can you quickly find a partner and *form* a single-file line?

2. Let's see how quickly the person in the back can *step* to the front of his or her partner.

3. How else can the person in the back *move* to the front of his or her partner (e.g., a *hop*, a *jump*)?

4. Try it again using another way to move.

5. Which set of partners can take turns *moving* to the front from the back until they have touched the opposite wall (or opposite end of the playing area)?

Whole-Group Learning Experience:
NO "BODY" IS LAST: Tell the children that today they will use their bodies to play a group line activity. Divide the children into groups of five or six. Ask each group to form a single-file line. Instruct the children in each line to either place their hands on the shoulders or the waist of the person standing in front of them.

On the teacher's signal, the child at the back of the line chooses a way to move his or her body to the front of the line. The action continues until the entire line formation has moved to the opposite side of the playing area.

For a greater challenge, encourage the children to try more complex movements such as skipping, jumping, hopping, a favorite animal walk, or a tumbling skill if floor mats are available. Allow enough space for each child to have a turn to move from the back to the front of the line.

Creative Closure:

1. What ways did you use to move to the front of the line? Show me.

2. Did it make any difference in the activity, "No 'Body' Is Last," if you were standing at the front or at the back of the line?

THE ENERGIZED BODY

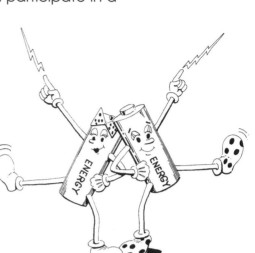

Primary Learning Objective: The child will imitate the movements associated with small objects that use batteries, and participate in a vigorous movement experience.

Materials or Equipment: None

Formation: Children are in their personal spaces.

Individual or Partner Learning Experience:
The teacher asks the following:

1. Who can tell me why we use batteries (e.g., to make things go)?

2. Show me what a battery looks like.

3. Can you use your body to *create* types of toys that use batteries (e.g., airplanes, trains, robots, trucks, remote control cars)?

4. Who can name an object in your home that uses batteries? Find a way to *move* your body like that object (e.g., clock's hands, flashlights).

5. Let me see how your body *moves* when it is feeling very strong and energized.

6. How does your body *move* when it is tired and needs to rest?

Whole-Group Learning Experience:
THE ENERGIZED BODY: Select one or more children to be "rechargers." All other children scatter throughout the playing area and assume the role of a non-working battery that must be "energized" by a recharger.

To do so, the rechargers run or gallop to each stationary battery. A battery is energized when a recharger crosses his or her hands and gently lays them on top of the battery. The recharger counts to three and says, "energized." At that moment, the energized battery moves throughout the playing area by pretending to be a race car. At some point, the child fatigues and finally stops. He or she remains stationary until a recharger approaches and re-energizes his or her battery.

After being recharged a second time, the child is free to move by pretending to be an airplane flying throughout the playing area. Upon fatiguing and stopping for the third time, the child is energized and moves like a train chugging throughout the playing area.

The teacher should see that a recharger also has a turn at being a battery before the movement experience is completed.

Creative Closure:

1. Our bodies need healthy foods to stay energized. Who can name some of these healthy foods?

2. Can you show me three different movements that tell me that our bodies are very strong and healthy?

HUMAN HELPERS

NASPE Learning
Standard #5

Primary Learning Objective: The child will discuss good versus evil character roles in a vigorous movement activity and demonstrate gestures reflecting friendship.

Materials or Equipment: None

Formation: Partners are scattered throughout the playing area.

Individual or Partner Learning Experience:
The teacher asks the following:

1. Who can *skip* arm in arm with their partner in general space?

2. Can you help your partner *jump* over an imaginary mud puddle?

3. Give your partner a light *pat* on the back to say, "Good job."

4. Pretend you are in a burning building. Show me how you would *help* a partner to safety. Switch roles.

5. *Shake* your partner's hand to show your appreciation.

Whole-Group Learning Experience:
HUMAN HELPERS: Divide the children into two groups. The children in one group are split into partners and form several caves when the two partners join hands. The caves scatter throughout the playing area. The other group pretends to be villains (e.g., well-known comic book, movie, or television characters). Designate two or more children to be the heroes and heroines.

Select a specific body part to be tagged (e.g., the right leg or the left shoulder). The heroes and heroines chase the villains, who flee from being tagged by standing underneath the raised hands forming caves. When a villain is tagged on the designated body part, he or she must switch roles with one of the children supporting the cave structure.

Creative Closure:

1. Who can give me examples of good versus bad behavior?

2. Show me one movement that represents friendship. Can you show me other gestures of friendship?

JUMPING JACKS AND JILLS

Primary Learning Objective: The child will successfully perform the mechanics involved in a Jumping Jack and, with a partner, share in the creation of an original exercise.

Materials or Equipment: A large sheet of paper and a marker

Formation: Children are in their personal spaces.

Individual or Partner Learning Experience:
The teacher presents the following:

1. Show me how you have learned to *jump* by using two feet and landing on your toes.

2. Who can *jump* forward, backward, and side-to-side?
   What part of your foot touches the floor first (toes)?
   Can you *wiggle* these body parts?

3. Today, we will demonstrate a very special exercise. It is called a "Jumping Jack" for boys, or a "Jumping Jill" for girls. Let's begin by making our bodies very stiff and narrow with our arms at our sides. Is it possible to *jump* up and open your legs in a triangle shape?

4. See if you can *clap* your hands over your head. Bring your arms back to your side. Now close the triangle.

5. If you are having problems coordinating your actions simply "flap your arms like a big bird."

Whole-Group Learning Experience:
JUMPING JACKS AND JILLS: Challenge partners to create or invent a new exercise. Suggest that the exercise involve bending, stretching, or curling the body into a shape. Partners should name their newly created exercise.

After a period of time, bring the children together. Encourage each set of partners to demonstrate their original exercise to the class. Challenge the whole class to perform the exercise two to three times, with the original two children observing and providing positive reinforcement or suggestions for correction.

List the names of the exercises on a large sheet of paper, or on a bulletin board for all the children to view and use in future classes.

Creative Closure:

1. During the Jumping Jacks and Jills, which body parts were the most difficult to control (hands or feet)?

2. How many of you found an exercise today that you would like to perform again at home? Show me.

CLEVER CREATIONS

Primary Learning Objective: The child will work collectively with his or her classmates to create large group shapes, and critique finished products.

Materials or Equipment: None

Formation: Children are scattered throughout general space.

Individual or Partner Learning Experience:
The teacher presents the following:

1. Show me what a rocket shape looks like.

2. Try to *build* a larger rocket using a friend's body.

3. Is it possible to be astronauts and to *move* your spacecraft from one place in the playing area to another place? Show me.

4. Let's end our space travel by using our bodies to *create* an object we see in the sky (e.g., moon, sun or star).

Whole-Group Learning Experience:
CLEVER CREATIONS: Inform the children that today's movement activity focuses on their ability to collectively use their bodies in the creation of large shapes. Reinforce the need to work cooperatively and to use everyone's body.

Select two to three children to be chasers. Before the action begins, the chasers must agree upon a large object that they would like to see built (preschool children may require suggestions like having a train or a tunnel built). The selected object is announced to the class (e.g., "We would like a castle built").

The remainder of the children scatter throughout the playing area. When an individual is tagged, he or she retreats to a designated area and assists the others in creating the object. After all the children are tagged, the chasers "inspect" the object by moving through, over, or around it.

Additional shapes include: an igloo, a fort, a school bus, a bridge, a racing car, a house, an ice cream shop.

Creative Closure:

1. In what ways did you need to change the shape as classmates joined you?

2. Which object was the most difficult to make? Why? Can you form one more group shape?

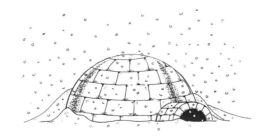

ON THE GO

Primary Learning Objective: The child will demonstrate the ability to move quickly, stop quickly, and perform a mature balance shape.

Materials or Equipment: None

Formation: Children are in their personal spaces.

Individual or Partner Learning Experience:
The teacher asks the following:

1. Who can *balance* on two different body parts at separate times without falling?

2. Can you *balance* on the hand you use to drink a glass of water? What about the foot you use to *kick* a ball?

3. See if you can *balance* on one foot while changing from a low to a high level.

4. Make the letter "O" with your arms while *balancing* on one foot.

5. Is it possible to *run* forward five steps, then *stop* quickly and maintain your balance? Try this movement three times.

Whole-Group Learning Experience:
ON THE GO: Challenge the children to imagine themselves as roadrunners. Explain that roadrunners are speedy birds found in California, Mexico, and Texas. They can obtain speeds up to 17 miles per hour by walking or running. These birds can grow up to two feet long.

This activity is a variation of the popular game, "Stork Tag." Begin by selecting one or more children to be a coyote (i.e., the chaser). Designate a specific shoulder to be tagged.

The remainder of the children pretend to be roadrunners and flee from the coyote. A roadrunner can avoid being tagged by balancing on one foot, folding the arms across the chest, and saying, "Meep, Meep." When a roadrunner is tagged, he or she cooperates with the coyote to tag other roadrunners.

Creative Closure:

1. What body parts helped you to stop quickly and maintain your balance?

2. Who can think of two different sports that require the athlete to balance? Use your body to move like athletes in those two sports.

HUMAN ARCHITECTURE

Primary Learning Objective: The child will maintain a compact shape while moving through obstacles of different heights and widths.

Materials or Equipment: None

Formation: Children are scattered throughout the playing area.

Individual or Partner Learning Experience:
The teacher presents the following:

1. Can you describe what an archway is, and the purpose it serves (e.g., provide pathways, ease of movement, and openness to space)?

2. Who can demonstrate how to make a strong human archway by standing and facing a partner, clasping your hands together, and extending them over your heads? (There should be space for a third child to move freely between the two bodies.)

Whole-Group Learning Experience:
HUMAN ARCHITECTURE: Divide the children into groups of three. Two of the three children should form an arch, while the third child is given an opportunity to practice locomotor skills through the archway. After each group member has completed the task, suggest that the two stationary partners lower the arch by kneeling. Encourage children to explore moving through the arch at this new height.

For a greater challenge, divide the children into two groups. One group uses their bodies to form strong arches of different heights, while the other group is challenged to move through them. Suggest that the arms can be held horizontally across the body, at a height of only two to three feet. Exchange roles.

Creative Closure:

1. Which body parts were the most difficult to keep close to your body when you were in a tiny compact shape?

2. What types of movements did you use when the height of the archway was lowered? Show me.

CHAPTER

Fostering Community Awareness through Movement

Fostering Community Awareness through Movement

Increasing the child's understanding of his or her local community is fundamental to the educational process. This understanding assists children in learning how their home environment differs from other home settings, and serves as a foundation for learning about other cultures in the upper-elementary school grades. Unlike early childhood specialists and classroom teachers who implement this content under the heading of social studies, geography, and history, physical educators have more often used the information as a way of expanding the child's movement  repertoire. In fact, the concept of community is most often discussed in wellness lectures that promote the use of community facilities, or when discussing consumerism in the middle and high school. This chapter makes use of the young child's previous knowledge of the local community, and offers all teachers of preschool through grade two children a variety of movement-based learning experiences to expand their existing curriculum.

The first series of activities in this chapter involve the class exploring community settings. They are presented according to individual and partner learning experiences, and whole-group learning experiences. The individual activities refer to those learning experiences performed by one child. The partner activities involve two children working dependently, and the whole-group activities involve the coordinated actions of three or more children.

Preschool specialists can compliment this chapter's content by providing the children with building block sets containing community workers, animals, and vehicles. For example, when implementing content regarding the role of construction workers and a construction site, the teacher can discuss the purpose of bridges and tunnels and how they are constructed. Ask the children to create these structures with building set materials. In dramatic play, the child can make use of child-size uniforms and props or dress-up clothing to spark creative role-playing possibilities. Preschool children are especially delighted when construction workers are invited to the childcare center and bring his or her tools for the children's viewing. Ask this individual to explain about the materials he or she uses in building houses. Show the difference between the types of nails, screws, bolts, and other fasteners used in building structures. Talk about the number of construction sites that exist near the school. Ask the children if they live in a new house, an apartment building, or in a house that has been repaired, expanded, or changed.

In keeping with the construction example, teachers who work with kindergarten children can challenge them to draw objects that are seen at the construction site (e.g., trucks, cars, cranes, bulldozers). Kindergarten children have the cognitive capacity, and are curious about the roles that different adults play, unlike the preschool child who tends to be more fascinated with the workings of objects. Storybooks serve as wonderful props for children in grades one and two. Ask the children to role-play the actions of the main character (e.g., a construction worker, a foreman). Select a storybook containing vivid pictures of objects or things. Challenge the children to differentiate between those objects that are man-made and those objects that are natural in nature.

The second series of learning experiences introduces the child to the actions and behaviors of community roles. Each learning experience reflects NASPE's National Standard Two for K-12 Physical Education. The primary learning objective is for all children to repeat the actions and imitate the behaviors of common community workers and helpers. Simple classroom props can be used to enhance the child's motivation for active participation. All learning experiences in this section take place in each child's personal space. The chapter ends by offering a series of movement narratives reflecting unique community settings, and several holiday activities celebrated in the community.

The following story is intended to assist the child's understanding of how communities were formed and have continued to grow. It can also serve as an introduction to the series of learning experiences that follow.

BUILDING BLOCKS OF A COMMUNITY

Many years ago, animals *roamed* freely through open fields and deep forests *searching* for food and fresh water. After the animals found a drinking hole in a pond, a lake, or river, they would return each day, *trekking* back and forth between their feeding area and the water. As time passed, pathways were formed by the *tramping* hooves and paws of animals. Buffalo and deer *wandered* across America, and their paths formed trails along the plains and through the mountain areas.

These pathways or trails were used by the Native Americans and became the first roads for the early pioneers as they *cut* more underbrush to widen the trails. Some families settled along these roads and *built* their homes. As more people settled, they needed a place to buy, sell, or trade their goods, like vegetables for tools. A market area was formed where two roads crossed so that people could come from more than one direction. These two roads would later become "Market Street" and "Main Street" for many towns and cities throughout our country. The first streets in New York City, for example, were made from trails used by Native Americans. Many of the *crooked* streets in Boston were made from cow paths.

Soon other settlers began to *build* shops in order to *repair* their tools and *mend* their clothing. As more shops and houses were built, the *footsteps* of people made pathways or streets in the same way the earlier animals had made pathways in the forest. Some pathways *twisted* around buildings, ponds, and hills. Visitors to the town *followed* the twisted street that ran alongside the buildings and sometimes got lost. Thereafter, town planners were called to ensure that streets would be laid in straight lines. Some streets were parallel to each other, which means they ran in the same direction. Others crossed and were perpendicular to each other. Over time, each street was named on a sign post, and covered with stones and bricks so that wagon wheels could more easily turn. Later, they were paved with asphalt for cars and other vehicles.

(cont.)

As people *built* more homes, the number of streets increased. Towns and neighborhoods included schools, farms, grocery stores, laundries, pet stores, and even pizza parlors. Recreational features included family parks, zoos, and toy shops. The desire to travel from town to town and from city to city encouraged people to *build* train stations, airports, garages, and car washes. Construction sites increased, and fire stations protected people and their homes. As more people moved into the community, the population of people increased and special trades were added until each community developed unique characteristics.

Following the story, the teacher should stress that all communities have unique buildings and offerings. The movements that take place within each community, however, are similar, and can be learned and copied. Explain that they can use their bodies and pretend to move like the objects or things seen in their community. Teachers can also stress that as the children use their bodies to explore the movements of a community, they should think of their own home setting and community, and the very special movements they see or experience each day.

THE COMMUNITY FARMHOUSE

Primary Learning Objective: The children will name and imitate the sounds and movements common to barnyard animals.

Materials or Equipment: None

Formation: Children are in their personal spaces.

Individual or Partner Learning Experience:
The teacher presents the following:

Farms consist of large areas of land that can be used to grow food and raise animals. The first farmers raised just enough crops to feed their families. They used wooden plows pulled by horses.

1. Farmer Seekins awakens early in the morning to milk the cows. Help him by *squatting* down and *sitting* on the milking stool. Show me the movement we use to milk the cows.

2. Let's *throw* feed to the baby chicks.

3. Farmer Seekins enjoys plowing the garden. Pretend to *drive* the tractor through the rows of vegetables. *Grasp* the steering wheel tightly as you *move* over the bumpy land.

4. Can you use one arm to show me how a tractor *plows* the land?

5. Make-believe you are using a shovel and *dig* a hole. Now *plant* a seed and *cover* it with dirt.

6. Demonstrate the action of a sprinkler watering the garden. *Stretch* your body upward like the vegetables when they grow.

7. Try to *lift* bales of hay from the fields. *Place* the bales on a large truck.

8. Who can *pump* water from a deep well?

9. Can you *skip* along a berry patch? *Stoop* low to the ground to *fill* a basket of strawberries.

(cont.)

Whole-Group Learning Experience:
A FARMYARD: Tell the children that they can use their bodies to form a farmyard fence. Begin by dividing the children in two groups. One group uses their bodies to form the fence. To form the fence, they must stretch upwards and stand very still. The remaining children should stand inside the fence and name and perform the movements of their favorite barnyard animals. Exchange roles.

Creative Closure:

1. Who can name your favorite action that you performed today?

2. Copy me as I pretend to use a hammer to fix the barn door. Who can make-believe that one of the walls in this room is the barn door?

THE COMMUNITY FIRE STATION

Primary Learning Objective: The children will demonstrate activities common to a fire station.

Materials or Equipment: Red or orange streamers, bubblewrap, paper plate, rope

Formation: Children are in their personal spaces.

Individual or Partner Learning Experience:
The teacher presents the following:

The fire station holds the fire trucks and provides a house where the firefighters eat and sleep. The men and women are always ready to move quickly when the alarm rings.

1. *Grasp* the cord and *ring* the fire bell.
   This sound tells the firefighters that there is a fire.

2. How quickly can you *pull* on your boots, *slip* into your fire coat, and *strap* on your helmet?

3. Can you slide down the pole and *hurry* to the truck? Use your hands to *grasp* the pole.

4. What color is the fire engine (red, lime green, or yellow)?
   Show me how you can *move* quickly like a fire truck. *Honk* the horn. *Make* the sound of the siren.

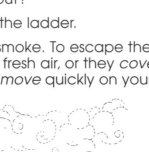

5. *Pretend* you are using the fire hose. Who can show me how the water *rushes* through the hose to put the fire out?

6. Use your arms and legs to *climb* the ladder.

7. Sometimes rooms are filled with smoke. To escape the smoke, the firemen and fire women either use a mask to get fresh air, or they *cover* their faces and *move* quickly along the floor. Can you *move* quickly on your hands and knees through a smoke-filled room?

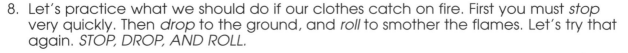

8. Let's practice what we should do if our clothes catch on fire. First you must *stop* very quickly. Then *drop* to the ground, and *roll* to smother the flames. Let's try that again. *STOP, DROP, AND ROLL.*

(cont.)

9. Can you and a partner use your bodies to *make* a fire truck? One child *steers* the fire truck while the other child *rings* the bell.

Whole-Group Learning Experience:
A FIREHOUSE LADDER: Explain to the children that they can use their bodies to form a giant ladder along the floor. One child needs to lie face down on the floor and stretch his or her body into a long shape. The next child should lie down and grab that child's ankles. The next child in line connects until a long ladder shape is created.

PUTTING OUT THE FIRE: Divide the children into two groups. Group one is given red or orange streamers to wave, and a sheet of bubble wrap to stomp on to make the crackling sound of fire. Group two represents a fire engine by forming a single-file line and holding a rope symbolizing the firehose. The first child in line holds a paper plate as a steering wheel. The second child in line is given a sheet of paper representing a map to the fire. The fire engine maneuvers throughout the playing area until coming upon the fire where the hose is used to extinguish the imaginary flames. The flames die down to a low level.

Creative Closure:

1. What kinds of things can we do to prevent fires in our home?

2. Is it possible to create a giant water hose using our bodies?

THE COMMUNITY TOY SHOP

Primary Learning Objective: The children will make-believe their bodies have become their favorite playthings.

Materials or Equipment: None

Formation: Children are in their personal spaces.

Individual or Partner Learning Experience:
The teacher presents the following:

Toys are objects created for the enjoyment of children.

1. Let's begin by using our bodies to move like several favorite toys. Who can show me how to *spin* like a top?
2. Can you pretend to *wiggle* a Hula-Hoop around your waist?
3. How high can you *bounce* your body into the air like a rubber ball?
4. Jumping rope helps the heart grow stronger. Make-believe you are *jumping* rope.
5. The wooden toy rowboat has two oars. *Raise* your arms and pretend to *row* the boat down the river.

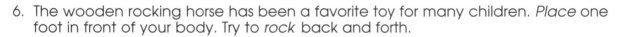

6. The wooden rocking horse has been a favorite toy for many children. *Place* one foot in front of your body. Try to *rock* back and forth.

7. The ballet dancer *stretches* upward and *walks* on his or her toes. Find a way to *walk* on your toes and *twirl* around like the dancer.
8. Show me how you can *march* like a toy robot.

(cont.)

9. Let's pretend to *strap* on a pair of ice skates. Can you *slide* and *move* as if you were *skating* on slippery ice?

10. Show me that you can *jump* very high with a pogo stick. *Raise* your body to *spring* upward like the pogo stick.

11. Superhero dolls wear costumes in their adventure roles. Pretend to *step* into your costume and show me how *strong* you can make your body.

12. Toy rockets blast off on a count of ten. Ready, *lower* your body and then *spring* upward like a rocket.

Whole-Group Learning Experience:

A JILL- OR JACK-IN-THE-BOX: Explain to the children that they can use their bodies to form a large Jill or Jack-in-the-Box. Some of the children form the box by standing side-by-side to make a square. Within the box is a group of children who stoop low to the floor like a folded Jack or Jill. These children grasp their knees while balancing on their toes as they stoop. One child must stand outside the box to crank the handle as the box children say:

> Jack-in-the-Box
> Jill-in-the-Box
> *Tucked* down in your box today,
> We'll *crank* the handle so you'll
> Come out and *PLAY*

The Jills- and Jacks-in-the-Box spring upward on the word "Play." Switch roles.

A DOLL'S HOUSE: Tell the children that they can combine four bodies to form a doll house. Begin by having each group of four children make a square. Ask the children to kneel down on their knees, and extend their arms upward. The children should grasp the wrists of the person across from them to make the roof of the house.

SCOOTERS: It takes two bodies to form a make-believe scooter. One child stands very tall and places his or her fists on the chest. The other person stands behind this person, and grasps the first child's elbows. Partners move forward by taking sliding steps while not bumping other sets of partners. Exchange roles.

A LITTLE RED WAGON: Wagons carry boys' and girls' toys. Groups of three can form a wagon that moves forward. Two children face each other and grasp wrists. The third child acts as a handle and pulls the cart along. Exchange roles.

Creative Closure:

1. Who can identify a different toy we did not see today and show us how it moves?

2. Build a large toy using a partner's body.

THE COMMUNITY PARK

Primary Learning Objective: The children will remember former experiences, and demonstrate a variety of ways of moving outdoors.

Materials or Equipment: None

Formation: Children are in their personal spaces.

Individual or Partner Learning Experience:
The teacher presents the following:

We can use our imaginations and make-believe that we are at our community park.

1. Let's *move* like the animals we see in the park. Can you *scamper* along the ground like a squirrel? Use your hands and feet to *move* quickly.

2. *Point* to a robin's nest. The young birds have hatched. Pretend to be a baby robin and *stretch* your brand new legs. Sometimes your legs *wobble* back and forth. You can pretend to *spread* your wings by *bending* your arms at the elbows. Now bring your hands to your shoulders. Can you *move* your wings back and forth in this position? *Hop* on one foot onto a branch. Now leave the nest and *flutter* your wings.

3. Is it possible to *move* like the animals that wiggle, crawl, slither, or creep along the ground? Can you *wiggle* along the ground like an earthworm? Show me another creature that *moves* along the ground (e.g., spider, snake, or bug).

4. Imagine that you are *flying* a kite that is tied to a long string. *Run* with one arm *held* over your head.

5. Can you *run* forward and pretend to *kick* a ball? Show me that you can *throw* a flying saucer disc, and then *run* and *snatch* it in the air.

6. *See* the people *playing* with bats and balls. Pretend to *catch* a ball that is hit high into the sky. *Run* and *chase* a ball that is rolling along the ground. *Stoop* to the ground to *pick* it up with your hands.
Can you pretend to *swing* a bat and *hit* the ball?

(cont.)

7. People exercise their muscles by running along a jogging path. Can you *run* or *jog* alongside a friend?

8. Our park also has a path for people to ride their bicycles. Pretend to *ride* a bicycle by *holding* onto the handle bars. *Lift* your knees high as you *ride* down the path.

9. Can you *lie* down on your back and *move* your legs to *pedal* a bicycle? Your legs can *pedal* quickly or slowly.

10. How quickly can you *pack* your picnic basket and *skip* home?

Whole-Group Learning Experience:
PARK BENCHES: Suggest to the children that they can use their bodies to form park benches. To do so, we must have two groups of children. One group will be the park benches by making box shapes. These shapes are scattered throughout the park. Children in the other group move vigorously, and then sit down gently on the benches for a short rest. Switch roles.

Creative Closure:

1. Can you tell me what your favorite outdoor activity is?

2. Find a way to move like your favorite activity.

THE COMMUNITY GROCERY STORE

Primary Learning Objective: The children will increase their awareness of items found in the grocery store, and assist a partner's movements in an imaginative whole-group learning experience.

Materials or Equipment: None

Formation: Children are in their personal spaces.

Individual or Partner Learning Experience:
The teacher presents the following:

1. Show me how your face *smiles* when you see a favorite food.

2. Can you use your body to show me the shape of different foods? Pretend to be a *tiny* green pea, a *long* ear of yellow corn, a *bumpy* potato, a *round* green head of lettuce, a *large* loaf of bread, and a *thin* orange carrot.

3. Let's *move* through the different sections of the grocery store. What does your body look like if you are *shivering* in the frozen food section?

4. Mexican food can taste very hot. How would you *move* after eating a hot red pepper?

5. The vitamin section helps you to grow strong. *Make* yourself into a *strong* shape.

6. We can use our bodies to make a large bowl of jelly beans. Jelly beans are many different colors. Who can *make* the small *oval* shape of the jelly bean? Let's *squeeze* together and form a large bowl of jelly beans.

Whole-Group Learning Experience:
SHOPPING CARTS: Explain that the children can use their bodies to form the shape of a shopping cart. Ask them to place their arms in front of their body to make the basket. Have them move through the aisles while holding their arms forward. Work with a partner and push a shopping cart. One child needs to make the basket with his or her arms. The other partner stands behind the basket and pushes the cart. Move through the aisles of the grocery store without touching other shopping carts. Exchange roles.

Creative Closure:

1. Can you name five healthy foods found in the grocery store?

2. Who can draw their favorite food in the air?

THE COMMUNITY PET STORE

Primary Learning Objective: Children will exhibit the movements of common pets.

Materials or Equipment: None

Formation: Children are in their personal spaces.

Individual or Partner Learning Experience:
The teacher presents the following:

Remind the children that we need pet stores to help us take care of our family pets.

1. Can you pretend to *cradle* a kitten in your arms? *Rock* your arms back and forth.

2. There is a turtle. Show me how you can *move* close to the ground like a turtle.

3. Look at the puppies learning to walk. Who can *move* quickly on your hands and feet?

4. Is it possible to *slither* on the floor like the snake in the tank?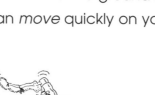

5. The parakeet loves to fly. See if you can *flap* your arms like wings. *Fly* carefully around our playing area.

6. The lizard moves very quickly to hide behind a rock. Let's *make* the movement of a lizard with a partner. One of you will *crawl* like the lizard and the other will *stand still* like a rock. Take turns at being the lizard and the rock.

Whole-Group Learning Experience:
A FISHBOWL: Tell the children that they can use their bodies to make a giant fishbowl. Some children will be the bowl, and some will be the fish. Ask who would like to be part of the giant fishbowl? These children must join hands and form a large circle. Everyone must hold hands or the water will escape. The other children can step into the circle. They use their bodies to move like fish by placing both arms behind their backs. See who can bend forward and swim like goldfish. Exchange roles.

Creative Closure:

1. What if you could choose any pet. What would it be?
2. Explore other ways to move like pets.

THE COMMUNITY GAS STATION AND GARAGE

Primary Learning Objective: The children will use their bodies to perform the actions associated with a gas station and car garage.

Materials or Equipment: None

Formation: Children are in their personal spaces.

Individual or Partner Learning Experience:
The teacher presents the following:

1. Can you use your body to *make* the shape of a car?

2. Use your arms to show me the *movement* of the windshield wipers.
3. Show me how you would use the steering wheel to *move* in different directions.
4. Is it possible to *make* the shape of your car's tires?
5. Your car's motor has pistons that move up and down. Show me this up and down *movement* as you pretend to *drive* along.
6. Like your body, your car needs fuel to keep moving. Let's *skip* to a make-believe gasoline station to refuel your car.
7. Who can show me the *shape* of a gasoline pump?

8. Who can *dangle* their arm like a gas pump hose?

(cont.)

9. When cars run out of gas, a tow truck is called. Can you and a friend take turns *towing* each other's car? Your hand can be the hitch that *tows* the car.

10. The person at the garage is called a mechanic. He or she tunes your car's motor. Can you *move* like a motor that needs repair? Make the sound of a motor that needs repair.

11. Use your arm like a jack that *lifts* your car up into the air.

12. Can you *lie* on your back and use your legs to *move* under a car to make repairs?

Whole-Group Learning Experience:
REFUELING: Tell the children that they can use their bodies to play a game. Divide the children into two groups. One half of the group are gas pumps and stand very still along one side of the room. They use their arms to form the gas hoses. The remainder of the children pretend to steer their cars throughout the playing area. When the driver needs more gas, he or she moves to a pump and says, "Please fill it up." The children can refuel their car any time to keep moving. When their car is no longer able to move quickly, they can exchange places with a gas pump.

Creative Closure:

1. What foods make the best fuel for a healthy body?

2. Who can form a motorcycle with a friend and drive throughout our playing area?

3. How many times did you need to refuel your body's car?

THE COMMUNITY TRAIN STATION

Primary Learning Objective: The children will interact cooperatively as they explore three different ways to move like a make-believe train.

Materials or Equipment: None

Formation: Children are in their personal spaces.

Individual or Partner Learning Experience:
The teacher presents the following:

1. Show me how the big clock outside the ticket station *moves* its hands.

2. Is it possible to *move* your arms like the wheels of a train?

3. *Use your arms* to show me how the railroad track signal *blocks* cars.

4. Let's pretend we are repairing the railroad tracks. Can you *swing* a heavy hammer and *drive* spikes into the ground?

5. Who can use his or her body to *make* the shape of a boxcar? Your legs, arms, and back can be used to make this shape.

6. *Stand* and *make* the movement of the train. *Blow* the whistle as you chug along.

7. Can you say, "chug-chug, clickity-clack, here we go around the railroad track," as you *move* along?

8. *Wave* good-bye to your friends as you *chug* along.

Whole-Group Learning Experience:
THE CHUG-ALONG TRAIN: Tell the children that they can form a group train by finding three or more friends. Create the train by putting their hands on the next child's shoulders. Chug along the tracks.

CHUG A CHUG A CHOO CHOO TRAIN: Ask the children to make a group train by placing their hands on the next child's waist. Chug along the tracks.

(cont.)

TUG AND CHUG: Explain that the children can form a group train by holding on to the next child's elbows. Move along the tracks together.

TRAIN TUNNELS: Ask the children to use their bodies to form make-believe tunnels for trains to move through. Some children will use their bodies to make tunnels by joining hands to form a high arch shape. The other children can make group trains and travel through the tunnels. Exchange roles.

Creative Closure:

1. How many different body parts did we use today to make our train?

2. Is it possible to make a large group tunnel for a small train to move through?

THE COMMUNITY CAR WASH

Primary Learning Objective: The children will explore and identify various movements and actions related to a car wash.

Materials or Equipment: None

Formation: Children are in their personal spaces.

Individual or Partner Learning Experience:
The teacher presents the following:

1. Before we have our car washed, we should *vacuum* the inside to remove dirt. Can you pretend to *push* a vacuum cleaner along the floor? *Push* and *pull* the vacuum cleaner along the floor.

2. Pretend to use a sponge and *wash* the tires of the car. Your body should be at a low level near the ground.

3. Can you *spin* around like the brushes you see in a car wash?

4. Large rollers are used to move the car through the car wash. Can you use your arms in front of your body to *make* a rolling movement? Try making small circles with your arms *stretched* out at your sides.

5. Is it possible to *hold* your arms in a circular shape and *move* like the soap bubbles that clean the car?

6. Show me how the water *sprays* all over the car.

7. Imagine you have a large towel to dry the car. *Stretch* and *reach* to dry the roof. Use both hands to *make* a circular movement with the towel.

(cont.)

8. Make-believe you are *polishing* the car's chrome.

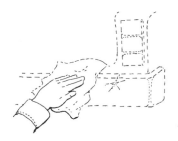

Whole-Group Learning Experience:

A CAR WASH: Divide the children into two groups. Explain to the children that they can use their bodies to form a long car wash. One group will need to be the two walls of the car wash. These children should stand side-by-side. They use their arms to make rollers in front of their bodies. The remaining children drive their cars through the car wash. Exchange roles.

Additional Props: For added creativity, props can be added to this car wash movement learning experience. Try using pompoms as brushes, bubbles as soap, jump ropes or short pieces of a clothesline to represent water hoses, and sponges or towels to dry off the newly washed cars. The teacher holds red and green circular pieces of construction paper to signal when the cars are to advance or stop at stations while traveling through the car wash. Children are divided into five groups.

Creative Closure:

1. Name two other objects that keep things clean in our community.

2. Let's see your bright and shiny car. Can you start the motor and grasp the steering wheel to drive home? Drive carefully and don't bump other cars.

THE COMMUNITY PIZZA PARLOR

Primary Learning Objective: The children will combine their bodies to create a popular family food.

Materials or Equipment: None

Formation: Children are in their personal spaces.

Individual or Partner Learning Experience:
The teacher presents the following:

1. Who can tell me what pizza dough is made from (e.g., flour)?

2. Let's pretend to make a pizza. To begin, everyone must imagine a large lump of pizza dough. Can you *roll* your pizza dough with a rolling pin? *Move* it from hand to hand. Can you *make* it flat? Show me how you would *make* the dough smooth. Try to *throw* the dough above your head and *catch* it.

3. We need tomato sauce. Is it possible to *make* our bodies very flat like the pizza sauce on the dough?

4. What toppings can we add to the dough? Who can *make* a round pepperoni circle with their body? Discover a way to *shape* your body like *narrow* slivers of cheese? Mushrooms look like little stools when they are picked. Show me how you can *stoop* low to the ground like a mushroom.

Whole-Group Learning Experience:
A LARGE PIZZA PIE: Challenge the children to use their bodies to form a large pizza pie. Divide the class into three groups. Ask one group to lie down and form the outside crust with their friends. This is a large circle shape. The second group of children become slivers of cheese, round pepperoni shapes, tiny mushrooms, or pizza sauce. To cook the pizza, the third group of children run around the outside and make the pizza very hot. Complete the activity by having all of the children run and skip around the shop while the pizza cools.

Creative Closure:

1. Who can use their body to create another pizza topping?

2. Now try to combine your body with a partner's to make a pizza shape.

THE COMMUNITY CONSTRUCTION SITE

Primary Learning Objective: The children will manipulate classmates' bodies to perform movements similar to those found in a construction site.

Materials or Equipment: None

Formation: Children are in their personal spaces.

Individual or Partner Learning Experience:
The teacher presents the following:

1. Can you pretend you are a very tall building by *stretching* upward?

2. *Put on* a hardhat to protect your head. Use your arms and legs to *climb* the steel ladder.

3. Is it possible to *walk* along a narrow steel beam without falling off? *Place* your arms out at the side of the body to help you *balance.*

4. Show me how you can *walk* with giant steps to *move* from beam to beam.

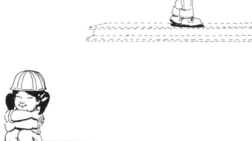

5. Let's *move* our body like an elevator down to the ground level.

6. Pretend to *unload* tools from a large truck. Use your body to *show* me how heavy the tools feel.

7. Can you *lift* a heavy tool by using your leg muscles? Slowly *lower* your body and *place* your arms around the bottom of the large tool. Now *lift* the tool by *raising* your leg muscles. This movement prevents you from injuring your back.

8. Imagine your body is a jack hammer breaking the concrete. You need to *jump* up and down on two feet very quickly to make the movement of a jack hammer.

9. Find a way to *make* a noise like a drill and *spin* around in a circle.

10. The cement mixer has a large container. It churns cement, gravel, sand, and water to make concrete. Can you use both arms to *imitate* the turning movement of the mixer? See if you can *turn* your whole body like the cement mixer.

11. Wheelbarrows are used to carry tools and dirt. Let's work with a friend to make the shape of the wheelbarrow. One child should *lie* on his or her back. The partner *holds* the ankles to make the handles of the wheelbarrow.

12. Pretend you are a bulldozer *pushing* dirt. Find space along a wall and *push* while making the sound of the bulldozer.

Whole-Group Learning Experience:

A HOUSE: Explain to the children that the word construction means "building." Challenge the children to use their bodies to form a house. Ask them to stand very tall and become the walls of the house. Add more children and make the door or archway into the house. Decorate the outdoors by having some children pretending to be trees, hedges, or flowers in a flower bed.

Creative Closure:

1. Who can recall three different movements common to a construction site?

2. Who would like to help build a neighbor's house? With your friends, show me how this could be done.

THE COMMUNITY LAUNDROMAT

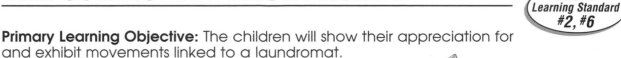

Primary Learning Objective: The children will show their appreciation for and exhibit movements linked to a laundromat.

Materials or Equipment: None

Formation: Children are in their personal spaces.

Individual or Partner Learning Experience:
The teacher presents the following:

1. Can someone tell me what we do in the laundry?

2. Who can *make* the sound of the washing machines?

3. Let's use our arms to *make* the shape of the soap bubbles.

4. Can you *twist* your hips like the movement of a washing machine?

5. Show me how you can use your feet to *stomp* out the dirt.

6. *Move* your body back and forth as if you were the clothing being washed.

7. Can you *spin* your body like the washing machine when it rinses the clothes?

8. Use your hands and pretend to *squeeze* the extra water out of the clothing.

9. Is it possible to *spin* your body very quickly like the clothes dryer?

Whole-Group Learning Experience:
A WASHING MACHINE: Explain that the children can use their bodies to make the movements of the washing machine. Some children need to stand in a large circle with their friends and make the movement of the washing machine. Other boys and girls stand in the middle of the washing machine and move like the clothing being washed. Still other children can pretend to be the soap bubbles. Make large, round soap bubbles with your arms. Challenge the children to try the movements together. Exchange roles.

Creative Closure:

1. It is important to care for your clothes. Pretend your hands are clothespins. Can you hang your shirt or blouse from the clothesline?

2. Can you fold your body in half like a bed sheet that is placed in the closet?

THE AIRPORT

Primary Learning Objective: The children will make-believe they are several objects that move quickly and fly.

Materials or Equipment: None

Formation: Children are in their personal spaces.

Individual or Partner Learning Experience:
The teacher presents the following:

There are two types of airplanes. The first airplane can carry only one or two passengers because it has a small engine. This is called a single-engine airplane. The second type of airplane is very large and has two motors. It can carry many people to places around the world. This is called a passenger plane.

1. Can you *lie* on the floor and *make* an airplane shape with wings?

2. *Stand* and *place* your arms out to your sides to make a small airplane. Who can *imitate* the sound of the airplane's engine?

3. Show me how you can *run* and take off from a very long runway.

4. Find a way to *land* your small plane safely on the ground.

5. The helicopter is another type of small aircraft. Helicopters have a large propeller on top of them. When the propeller blades whirl around, they create a strong wind to lift the helicopter. Can you *spin* your arms like helicopter blades? Slowly *rise* upward into the air. Can you *travel* around our playing area while *spinning* slowly and not touching other helicopters?

6. The jet aircraft is built to move very quickly. Can you *make* the pointed nose of the airplane with your arms and *zoom* through our playing area?

(cont.)

7. We can use our bodies to form a large passenger plane that carries people to far away places. First, *stand* beside a partner. *Move* close together so that you are shoulder to shoulder. Can you *put* your arm around your partner's shoulders as good friends do? See if you can *move* together by using your two outside arms as wings. Let's practice air safety by making a long line of partner planes. Each plane should find a space to *stand* along the runway. On my signal, one plane *leaves* the runway and begins to *fly* through the skies. After the first plane has left the runway, a second plane may leave.

Whole-Group Learning Experience:
A PASSENGER PLANE: Explain to the children that they can also create a passenger plane. To build the passenger plane, two children stand behind two other children who are using their arms as wings. The front children are the pilots. The back two children place their hands on the shoulders of the pilots. Slowly, the four children move together pretending to fly to Europe.

Creative Closure:

1. Who can name different parts of an airplane and a helicopter?

2. Sometimes, airplanes fly in bad weather and strong winds. This is called bumpy air. Make-believe your airplane is flying in bumpy air.

THE COMMUNITY SCHOOL YARD

Primary Learning Objective: The children will imitate the movements and actions associated with several large structures found in a school yard.

Materials or Equipment: None

Formation: Children are in their personal spaces.

Individual or Partner Learning Experience:
The teacher presents the following:

1. Can you *hop* on one foot through a hopscotch shape? Use your arms for balance as you *hop* through the make-believe boxes.

2. Use your arms and legs to *climb* up the make-believe monkey bars. What do you see at the top?

3. Who can use their arms and legs to crawl through an imaginary barrel?

4. Show me how you would *rock* your body back and forth like the movement of a swing. Pretend to give a friend a gentle *push*.

5. Imagine you are *gripping* the rungs of a horizontal metal ladder that has ten rungs. *Swing* from one rung to another while keeping a tight *grip*.

6. Let's use our bodies and *make* the movement of the seesaw. First, find a friend who is wearing a big smile. *Stand* so you can see your friend's smile. *Stretch* your arms in front of your body and *grasp* your partner's hands. *Hold* hands tightly. Take turns *standing* up and *stooping* down to make the movement of the seesaw.

(cont.)

7. We can also make a three-person seesaw. One child *makes* a wide stretched shape between two outside players. Both outside children *hold* a hand of the middle person and take turns *moving* up and down.

Whole-Group Learning Experience:
A MERRY-GO-ROUND: Tell the children they can use their bodies to make the movement of a merry-go-round. This is possible by finding three friends. These three friends must stand back to back in a circle shape. Each child's arms need to be straight out in front of the body. Move very slowly around and around and up and down. Stop the merry-go-round so that other riders can join the children. Additional children can stand between the arms that make the sections of the merry-go-round. Encourage the children to move together safely. (To make a large merry-go-round, one half of the class grasps hands to form a large circle. Everyone faces towards the center of the circle. The remaining children place one hand onto the shoulder of a circle person. The children all move in the same direction as the merry-go-round slowly moves in a circle shape.)

A SCHOOL BUS: School buses drop children off at the school yard. Ask the children to quickly stand beside a partner and hook elbows. Make a long line with partners standing behind each other. Invite the children to place their outside hand on the shoulder in front of them? Slowly move forward.

Creative Closure:

1. Who can name three different movement skills that we performed on our imaginary school yard?

2. Is it possible to design a totally new piece of equipment with a group of friends?

HOUSEKEEPERS

It is a housekeeper's responsibility
to keep other people's homes tidy and clean.

1. Let's use our hands and pretend to *dust* the furniture. *Stretch* and *dust* the cobwebs from the ceiling.
2. Imagine that you are *pushing* a large vacuum along the floor. Now *shake* the rugs in the breeze to remove the dirt.
3. How quickly can you *pick* up five toys and *place* them in a toy box? Can you *fold* three pieces of clothing and put them in a drawer? *Grab* the blankets and *pull* them forward to make the bed.
4. Show me how you can *stretch* upward to *wash* the windows.
5. Sometimes housekeepers shop for food in the market. Try to *fill* a make-believe shopping cart with healthy foods from the top shelf. *Lower* your body to the middle shelf. *Stoop* downward and *fill* your cart from the lower shelf.

HOUSE PAINTERS

House painters use paint buckets and brushes
to make buildings more beautiful.

1. Can you *step* into a pair of overalls? *Pull* on gloves to protect your hands and *slip* on a small cap to cover your hair.
2. Let's *throw* a large tarp or drop cloth over the furniture. Now use a make-believe scraper to remove the old paint.
3. *Open* the bucket and *mix* the paint with a circular motion. *Dip* your brush into the bucket and *paint* the walls a bright sunny color.
4. Discover how to use up and down strokes. Try *using* a paint roller for long smooth strokes. *Paint* long lines on the floor.
5. Finish the paint job by showing me how you can *climb* up a ladder to the ceiling. *Stretch* and *paint* the ceiling over your head.

POLICE OFFICERS

Police officers enforce laws to keep people safe from crime.

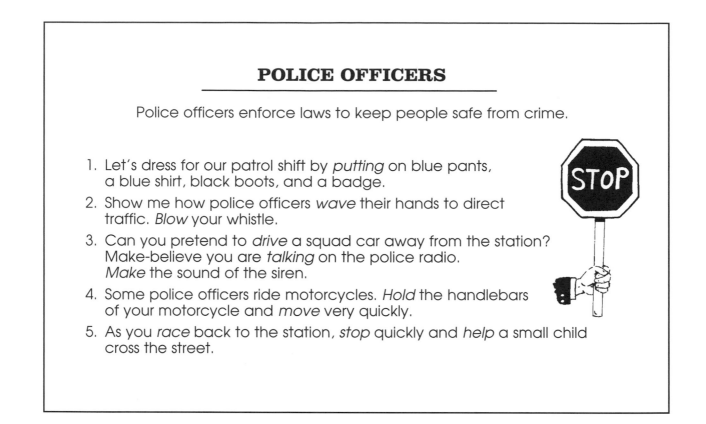

1. Let's dress for our patrol shift by *putting* on blue pants, a blue shirt, black boots, and a badge.
2. Show me how police officers *wave* their hands to direct traffic. *Blow* your whistle.
3. Can you pretend to *drive* a squad car away from the station? Make-believe you are *talking* on the police radio. *Make* the sound of the siren.
4. Some police officers ride motorcycles. *Hold* the handlebars of your motorcycle and *move* very quickly.
5. As you *race* back to the station, *stop* quickly and *help* a small child cross the street.

BUS DRIVERS

It is the bus driver's job to
transport people safely from one place to another.

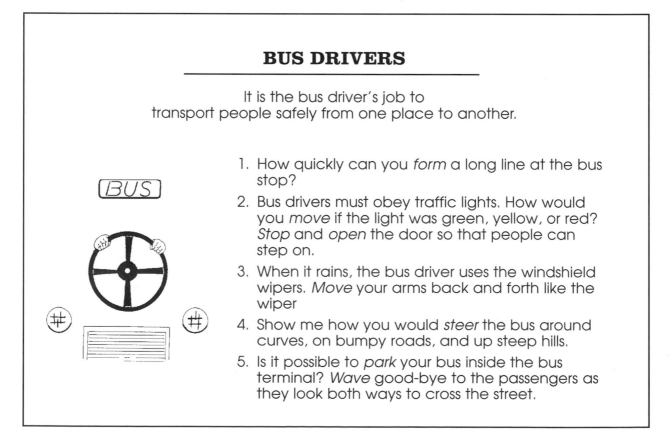

1. How quickly can you *form* a long line at the bus stop?
2. Bus drivers must obey traffic lights. How would you *move* if the light was green, yellow, or red? *Stop* and *open* the door so that people can step on.
3. When it rains, the bus driver uses the windshield wipers. *Move* your arms back and forth like the wiper
4. Show me how you would *steer* the bus around curves, on bumpy roads, and up steep hills.
5. Is it possible to *park* your bus inside the bus terminal? *Wave* good-bye to the passengers as they look both ways to cross the street.

SHOEMAKERS AND COBBLERS

Many years ago, the Egyptians used four people to make one pair of shoes. It was the first person's job to stretch the leather. The second person cut out the soles of the shoes, and the third person punched holes for the laces. The job was complete when the fourth person used thin strips of leather to string the laces. Shoemakers today still work with leather to create a pair of shoes.

1. Pretend you have one large piece of leather. *Stretch* the leather on one side of your body and then the other.
2. Use your finger to *trace* around the soles of your shoes. Use make-believe scissors to *cut* around the soles.
3. *Punch* holes in the leather where the laces will be placed. Take a giant needle and *sew* the leather together.
4. *Squeeze* the tube of glue that binds the shoe together. *Shine* your new shoes.
5. Show me what type of shoes you have made. How would you *move* if you were wearing heavy boots, tap-dance shoes, or jogging shoes?

TAILORS AND DRESSMAKERS

The materials we use to make clothing are made from fiber and threads that are woven into cloth. The sheep's wool (or fleece) is the most common animal fiber. Cotton is the most common plant fiber. Tailors and dressmakers design or mend clothing for people to wear.

1. Who can *measure* a friend's body to make a new coat? Pretend to use a tape measure and determine the length of the arms and shoulders.
2. *Trace* around the outline of the friend's upper body parts. This is your pattern.
3. Pretend your fingers are scissors and *cut* out the shape of the coat.
4. See if you can *thread* a make-believe needle and *sew* the pieces of fabric together. *Add* a few buttons and *tie* a knot at the end of the thread. Use an iron to *press* the new coat.
5. *Walk* around the playing area and *model* your new coat.

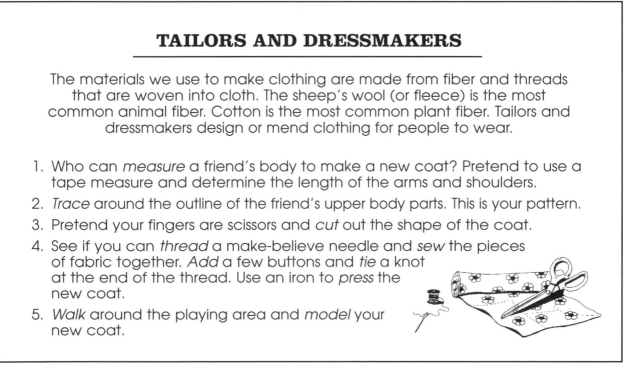

AMBULANCE DRIVERS

Ambulance drivers take injured or ill people to the hospital.

1. *Run* quickly and make the sound of an ambulance.
2. *Act* as if your arms are flashing lights and *make* those movements.
3. Stretchers are used to *carry* injured people. Find a partner and show me how you would *carry* a stretcher.
4. How do you help an injured person *walk* into the hospital?
5. The doctor listens to a person's heart with a stethoscope. *Move* to the sound that the doctor hears when listening to your heart.

BRICKLAYERS

Bricklayers prepare and lay brick to construct and repair structures such as walls, fireplaces, and chimneys.

1. Bricklayers or masons carry their materials in a wheelbarrow. *Fill* a make-believe wheelbarrow with bricks and *push* the wheelbarrow to a space where you can build a wall.
2. Show me how the bricklayer *mixes* cement.
3. *Lay* the bricks side-by-side to build a wall, a chimney, or a barbecue.
4. Bricks are laid on the wide flat sides, and cement or mortar is used between each brick to make a sturdy structure. Use a hand trowel to *smooth* the cement.
5. *Carry* the remainder of the bricks back to the construction site.

COWBOYS AND COWGIRLS

Cowboys and cowgirls often live on large ranches
and work with horses and cattle.

1. Cowboys and cowgirls use a rope called a lasso to round up cattle. Can you *swing* a lasso over your head and then *toss* it forward? See how many different ways you can *twirl* the lasso at the side of your body?

2. Cowboys and cowgirls like to cook their food outdoors on a large grill. Who can *gather* sticks of wood for a large campfire? *Stir* a large pot of chili with beans.

3. How can you *brush* your horse? Now *toss* on a saddle, *hold* on to the reins, and *gallop* along a path.

4. How would you *move* if you were *riding* a bucking bronco? *Wave* your cowboy or cowgirl hat and yell "Yahoo!"

5. Finish the day by *pulling* off your heavy leather boots.

ARTISTS

The first paintings were made by people drawing on cave walls. These drawings show hunters chasing and throwing spears at animals. Today's artists draw or paint pictures for people to display in their homes or buildings.

1. *Put* on a painter's apron to paint a large picture. Now *place* a huge canvas on an easel.

2. *Dip* your brush onto the palette of paints. Show me how you can *make* long, smooth strokes and wiggly lines. Can you *paint* a circle, a square, a rectangle, or a triangle? Is it possible to *paint* the outline of a person's body in the air?

3. Now *trace* a frame around your painting and *hang* it high on the wall for everyone to see.

4. Let's try working with fingerpaints. Copy me as I *swish* my hands into a can of finger paint. *Make* handprints along the floor. Can you *create* some fancy footprints along the floor? *Step* into the bucket each time you need more paint.

5. Pretend to *wash* your hands and feet, and then *shake* them dry.

ACTORS AND ACTRESSES

Actors and actresses entertain people by
playing roles on stage, on television, or in movies.

1. Who can *pretend* to be angry, sad, frightened, or clumsy?
2. Let's be famous characters in a fairy tale and *move* like wicked witches, brave knights, bashful dwarves, cowardly lions, or heroic princes and princesses.
3. How many different ways can you pretend to *laugh*?
4. Can you make-believe you are a curious spy and *creep* along the floor?
5. Actors and actresses use their whole body to show how they are feeling. What does your body look like when it is gloomy, silly, heavy, shy, jolly, or worried? *Clap* loudly and give yourself applause!

SCULPTORS

Sculptors wear smocks and use stone, clay, wood, and metal to
form shapes of people or things. The first sculptors modeled animal shapes in
bone and wood. Some sculptors made statues to look like famous people.

1. To carve a statue, the sculptor cuts into stone or a block of wood with sharp tools. Pretend to *move* a large piece of marble to a space in the playing area where you can create a statue. Use a hammer and a chisel to *shape* the statue. *Chisel* at the top, move to the middle area, and finish at the base.
2. In molding, the sculptor makes a model from soft clay, and then bakes the clay until it is hard. Find a way to *roll* a clump of clay into a round smooth ball. Is it possible to *make* it flat like a pizza pie? *Press* tiny holes into the clay.
3. Use a make-believe knife to *carve* a shape from wood. *Slide* the knife away from your body as you *carve* the shape.
4. Shapes or patterns that express feelings are called "abstract." Use your body to show me this kind of sculpture. Pretend to *bend* large pieces of steel into creative shapes. Let's *walk* around the playing area and *look* at all the creative shapes we've made today.

CLOWNS

Clowns have a very special job.
They try to make people laugh.

1. We can use our bodies to look and *move* like clowns. Let's begin by pretending to *paint* our faces. *Rub* on the makeup. *Draw* a large smile across your face. *Pop* on a large round nose.

2. Clowns have funny faces. *Show* me a happy clown face. Let's try a sad, long face. *Create* a goofy face.

3. Clowns wear colorful clothing. How would you *walk* if you were wearing large floppy shoes? Now *step* into large baggy pants. *Button* your striped and polka-dotted shirt, and *straighten* your large bow tie.

4. Can you *walk* low to the ground and *flap* your arms? What other ways can you use your body to make people laugh? Show me a big belly laugh.

5. We can use our bodies to *perform* make-believe tricks. Can you pretend to *play* a squeaky trumpet? *Blow* up a giant balloon. See if you can *walk* along a tight rope. *Run* and *jump* through a giant hoop. *Throw* confetti from a bucket. *Drive* a funny little car. Pretend to *toss* balls in the air and *catch* them. Find a way to *leapfrog* over another clown.

MUSICIANS

The first music was very different from the songs we hear today.
The sounds were made from sighs, clapping, moans, and shouts.

1. *Make* noises and let me hear what the first music might have sounded like.

2. The first musical instrument was the drum. Tribes of people many years ago used drums to drive away evil spirits. Drums are called percussion instruments because music is made by hitting them with sticks or hammers. Pretend to *beat* on a set of drums.

3. Musicians play wind instruments by *blowing* a hollow wooden or metal tube with holes cut into it. For some wind instruments, the fingers cover specific holes to make a musical note. Show me how you can *blow* into a blaring trumpet and *march* in a band. Who can make the *sliding* motion of a trombone?

4. Stringed instruments have strings stretched across a hollow box. Imagine you are *playing* the violin. Now *strum* on the strings of a guitar like a rock and roll guitar player.

5. *Move* like a conductor *leading* a large orchestra.

ARCHITECTS

The first great architects were Egyptians who built stone temples
and tombs. Today's architects use steel, glass, plastic, brick, concrete,
and other materials to make their designs.

1. Show me that you can *make* a wide, flat shape to represent the base or foundation of a large building.
2. Who can *make* an arch shape with their bodies?
3. How can you *stand* tall, like the columns that hold up a roof?
4. *Raise* your hands over your head to make the church steeples that point to the sky.
5. Can you *turn* your body to *make* the twisted spiral shapes seen at the tops of large skyscrapers?

TRANSPORTATION SPECIALISTS

The transportation specialist creates
rules so that people can travel safely to other
neighborhoods, cities, or states.

1. The earliest form of transportation was the horse. Pretend to *saddle* a horse and *gallop* throughout the playing area.
2. Ships with sails or oars were the next form of transportation. *Hold* both hands at a high level in front of your body like the sail on a small ship. Show me how you can *sail* in rough waters. Let me see you *make* the motion used to *row* a boat.
3. A large balloon filled with gas was the next means of traveling over the land. *Float* like a balloon.
4. The steamship and the steam railway were the next inventions. The first rail road trains were called "locomotives." *Chug* along a make-believe track.
5. The invention of the car made it possible for people to travel faster. Cars are made up of three basic units: the body, the engine, and the transmission. Imagine you are a sports car *moving* quickly on a track.
6. People strapped on wings and leaped off high buildings when they first tried to fly. They learned that a human's muscles are too weak to keep the body in the air. The invention of the airplane was made possible by the propeller. Make-believe your arms are propellers and *move* quickly throughout the playing area.

DANCERS

Thousands of years ago, people told stories by dancing. They danced to make the crops grow and to make it rain. Later, dancing became part of religious ceremonies. Today, dancers perform to entertain other people, and dance has become an art.

1. Ballet tells a story or conveys an idea or feeling. Classical ballet uses five basic positions from which all movements begin. Who can *place* their feet in five different positions?

2. Modern dance is based on free-flowing movements. See how many different ways you can *move* smoothly and gracefully.

3. Folk dancers wear colorful costumes and sometimes dance in a circle formation. Can you *place* both hands on your hips and *dance* in the shape of a circle?

4. In highland dances, performed in Scotland, the dancer moves to the music of bagpipes. *Point* the hand you wave toward the sky. The other hand is *placed* on your hip. Show me how you *kick* up your heels and *land* on your toes. *Bend* your knees to *land* safely.

5. Make-believe you are a famous ballroom dancer and *waltz* smoothly throughout the playing area.

PUPPETEERS

Puppets are small figures of animals or people that are manipulated by the hand or by strings. Puppets have been used in theaters in the East and West for hundreds of years.

1. In Asia, shadow puppets act out serious stories called drama. What kind of dramatic movements can you *make* with your face, feet, and hands?

2. There are puppets that fit over the hand. Glove puppets were first used in England. Pretend that both of your hands are glove puppets of your favorite animals. Have a conversation between the two puppets and *move* as the puppets suggest.

3. String puppets, called marionettes, were often used by traveling showmen who performed joyful and silly stories. How would you *move* if your arms and legs were attached to strings?

4. *Select* a friend and *create* a simple story. Pretend your bodies are puppets, and *act* out the story.

5. Find a friend and take turns pretending that one person is the marionette and the other person is the puppeteer. The puppeteer *pulls* make-believe strings to raise and lower the arms and legs of the puppet.

TRAVELING THROUGHOUT THE COMMUNITY

Paula *stretched* upward on her toes to look out the window.
She liked school, and she loved riding on the long yellow school bus.
Paula knew how much fun it was to travel from place to place. She enjoyed:

Walking to the movie theater,
Jogging to the park,
Running to the playground,
Galloping on horseback at the farm,
Pedaling her bicycle to the grocery store, and
Roller skating at the rink.

"Someday I will travel to far away places," thought Paula. She imagined:

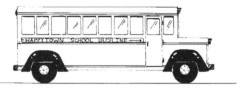

Driving a motorcycle along twisting roads,
Swinging on long vines in the jungle,
Chugging along railroad tracks,
Sprinting across the lake in a speedboat,
Trudging up a hill in a large tank,
Rocking back and forth on a sailing ship,
Riding a tall camel across the desert,
Blasting upward in a rocket to the moon, and
Parachuting from a plane.

At that moment, the school bus arrived at Paula's house. "Today, I will *ride* the elevator down, down, down, and travel on the bus to school," she said.

THE COMMUNITY ICE CREAM STORE

The ice cream truck parked alongside the neighborhood playground.
It was a white truck with one large window. Some children
hopped to the truck, others *galloped,* and still others *ran* as fast as
they could to select their favorite treats. These included:

stiff Popsicles®,
round scoops of ice cream,
long frozen bananas,
frosty milkshakes,
tiny chocolate sprinkles,
bubbling ice cream sodas,
soft ice cream cakes,
pointed waffle cones,

gooey chocolate fudge,
small red cherries,
thin strips of coconuts,
little pieces of nuts,
sticky caramel sauce,
plump strawberries,
soft marshmallows, and
light, fluffy whipped cream.

The children *stretched* upward on their toes to receive their favorite ice cream. They *shivered* from the cold, *smacked* their lips, and *rubbed* their stomachs before returning to the playground for a different type of treat.

THE COMMUNITY AMUSEMENT PARK

"Where are your shoes?" asked Billy's uncle. "You need to find your shoes if we are going to the amusement park." Billy *dashed* into the living room to search for his shoes. While *searching* he:

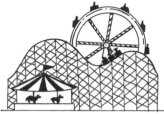

Crawled under the coffee table.
Skipped around the sofa,
Rolled his body over the rug,
Pranced two times around the piano.
Tiptoed behind the television, and
Collapsed into his favorite chair.

Billy's heart was beating quickly when his uncle brought him his shoes. "I hope your body is ready for an active day at the amusement park," said Billy's uncle, with a *silly* face.

On the ferris wheel, Billy *moved* in a large circular shape.
He *bobbed* up and down on the merry-go-round's moving horse, and
He *zoomed* to the top of a steel mountain on the giant roller coaster.
The mirrors in the funhouse made Billy look very *tall* and *skinny*, *short* and *wide*, and even *crooked*.
His body *whirled* around and around on the spinning cup ride.
He was *jerked* from side to side while steering a bumper car.
The haunted house made Billy *shake* and *tremble* with fear.
He *floated* in the clouds on the balloon ride,
Dangled over a cliff on the Daredevil ride, and ended the day by
Sliding down a long, steep water slide.

"That was great. My heart has been beating very fast all day," said Billy.

"Your heart is very fit," replied his uncle. "Let's see if it can pump faster," as he challenged Billy to a *race* home.

THE COMMUNITY SPORTS STADIUM

Julia and Justin waited quietly in line to pay for the tickets to the sporting event. The sports stadium was a giant round shape that contained many seats. People came to the stadium to watch players:

Jump high to shoot a basketball,
Kick a soccer ball down the field,
Swing a tennis racket at the side of the body,
Skate gracefully in the shape of the number eight,

GO TEAM !!

(cont.)

Catch a football with *outstretched* hands,
Leap in the air and then *roll* on a gymnastics mat,
Run very quickly in a track race,
And *dribble* a hockey puck down the ice.

Julia and Justin liked to see the players when they *patted* each other's back, *jumped* up and *slapped* hands, and gave each other *handshakes* at the end of the game.

Today, the two children would *yell* and *cheer*, *wave* their arms, and *clap* their hands for their favorite team.

Tomorrow, they would practice *running, hopping, jumping*, and all the movements in their favorite sport, so that someday people would come to watch them play in the sports stadium.

THE COMMUNITY HARDWARE STORE

Vinnie was fascinated with tools. He was always eager to watch his father build large houses for people to live in. Today, Vinnie was allowed to help. "With a little luck," said Vinnie's father, "We should be able to finish this project."

"A whole house!" thought Vinnie. "Boy, my father must be strong to build a whole house in one day!"

As Vinnie and his father entered the hardware store, his father turned toward Vinnie. "Let's play a game to help you learn about each tool," said Vinnie's father. Vinnie's father *stretched* upward to *reach* for the handsaw. Handsaws have very sharp teeth to cut lumber.

"*Show* me your sharp teeth," he said. "Now pretend to *saw* lumber by *pushing* one arm out in front of the body and *pulling* it back in. Do this five times."

Next, Vinnie's father said, "Drills are used for boring holes. *Spin* your body around three times like the movement of the drill. Pretend your arms are pliers and *squeeze* them together to grip the wood. Can you *twist* your whole body around and make believe you are a screwdriver?"

"What movement would your arm make if you were using a hammer?" asked Vinnie's father (pounding). "How would your body look if you were a nail being *pounded* into wood? Show me. Is it possible to *tighten* a nut and bolt with a wrench? Keep *twisting* the nut toward you."

"Almost done," said Vinnie's father. "We need to *rub* sandpaper back and forth to make the wood smooth. I can finish," he said, "If you can make the shape of a hook."

With that, Vinnie *curled* both arms to form the shape of a hook. "Why do we need a hook?" asked Vinnie.

"To hang this special bird house when we return home," replied his father.

"Of course, a bird house!" thought Vinnie. Vinnie could imagine a family of birds *flying* through the skies as his father *lifted* the ladder to the tree. Later, Vinnie was permitted to *climb* to the top and *place* the special house in the trees.

"During our next trip to the hardware store," thought Vinnie, as he *galloped* happily home, "I will learn about how to use the wooden sawhorses."

THE COMMUNITY ICE RINK

Willy *reached* and *stretched* for his ice skates. It was the first day of practice for his school's ice hockey team and Willy was late. He *ran* to school as fast as he could, leaving tiny penguin footprints in the snow. Willy's school had its own hockey rink called the Frosty Forum. He arrived just in time to *find* his own personal space for the team's daily stretches. He found a space where no one else was standing.

He *stretched* his body to *create* a wide shape, a twisted shape, followed by a narrow shape, and then *curled* his body into a tiny snowball shape. Coach Wally Walrus told the team it was important to warm the leg muscles. Everyone began to *run* and *pump* their arms while staying in their personal space. Willy could feel his heart pump faster. "Keep your head *upright* and your arms *close* to the sides of your body," said the coach.

Willy *stooped* downward and *laced* up his skates. He *slid* out onto the forum's ice and began to *skate*. He *skated* faster and faster, his little legs taking long strides. Soon Willy *spied* his two teammates Peter Polar Bear and Sylvia Seal. The three teammates *dashed* and *darted* throughout the ice rink without touching each other.

"I know!" said Willy, "We can also make pathways on the ice to get in shape!" The three friends *moved* in the shape of a triangle, a rectangle, a circle, and a figure eight.

"Let's try to *move* in the shapes of the letters of our first names," said Sylvia Seal. Willy *wobbled* along and made a letter "W" on the ice. Sylvia *skated* smoothly over the ice while making the letter "S," and Peter Polar Bear *plodded* along in the shape of a letter "P" for Peter.

Coach Wally Walrus *blew* the whistle to gather his team. The three friends *stopped* quickly and *skated* to the center of the rink. Everyone *sat* quietly as the coach talked about keeping their bodies healthy so that they could play their best. Willy *leaned* forward to *touch* his knees, his ankles, and his toes. He was feeling very happy and knew that it was going to be a good season.

THE COMMUNITY RACETRACK

Daniel took the white paper napkin that protected his ice cream cone and *crinkled* it in his hands. It was a perfect cloth to *rub* the chrome on the bright red racecar. "I want to be a race car driver when I grow up," thought Daniel.

From a distance, he could see Anna-Marie who was frantically *waving* and *jumping* up with excitement. She yelled, "Hurry Daniel, we need to find a seat in the bleachers."

Daniel *dodged* and *darted* through the crowd. He *climbed* up ten steps to sit with his sister. As he watched the cars drive closer to the starting line, he *closed* his eyes and thought what it would be like to be a world famous race car driver.

He thought about *strapping on* his helmet and safety belt, *turning* the key, and hearing the engine firing. The *trembling* of the car is making his hands *shake* on the vibrating steering wheel. Suddenly, the light turned green and the man *waved* the start flag. Daniel *extended* his leg and *slammed* on the gas pedal as the car *accelerated* to a high speed.

Weaving in and out, he began to *pass* other drivers. As he approached the lead car, he heard the crowd *cheering* and *clapping*. He wanted to finish in first place, so he *squeezed* the wheel and made an abrupt *turn* without touching any of the other cars. The car's tires were *spinning* as he *grabbed* the gear shift and *moved* it forward with one hand. The car was *shaking* as he moved closer to the finish line and *zipped* past all the other drivers. "I won! I won!" yelled Daniel, as he *waved* one hand in the air.

"What are you shouting about?" asked Anna-Marie, "The race hasn't even begun." The two children *sat* motionless, waiting for the start of *the* race. Anna-Marie slowly *leaned* back in her seat. The bright sun *hovered* over her head. Feeling very carefree, she *closed* her eyes and wondered what it would be like to be a famous female racecar driver.

THE COMMUNITY SHOESTORE

Lauren and Lucas's mother had promised the two children that they could each purchase one new pair of shoes during the Saturday shopping trip. Their shoe sizes were growing larger, like the rest of their bodies. A trip to the community shoestore had become a regular event. "What type of shoes will you buy Lauren?" asked Lucas. "I'm not sure, maybe I'll buy a pair of ballerina slippers so I can *twirl* and *whirl* around and around," said Lauren. "That would be fun," responded Lucas as he repeated the *movement.*

Both children remembered to be very polite when the salesperson asked how he could help. They had seen this man several times before. "May we please try on a pair of running shoes?" asked Lauren. The man quickly *climbed* ten rungs of the ladder to locate the children's sizes among the tall stack of boxes. The two children noticed that the shoes made them feel as light as a feather as they *sprinted* forward in the store's aisles. The man told the children that the first sneakers were black with a red dot at the heel. The sneakers had to be replaced when the little rubber circle on the heel faded, and then became ragged, and finally disappeared.

"May we try on a pair of basketball shoes?" asked Lauren. The salesperson *climbed* nine rungs of the tall ladder. These shoes came up high on the children's ankles for extra protection. The thin wedges of a basketball shoe were for grabbing a wooden court. Little suction cups on the sole prevented the children from slipping on the smooth wooden floors. Lucas began to *dribble* imaginary basketballs in a *zigzag* pattern and *take* fancy shots over his head. Lauren showed the salesperson how to *run* in place and *lift* the knees to get in shape for basketball.

"I'm really more interested in buying tennis shoes," said Lucas. So the salesperson *turned* around in a circle and *climbed* eight rungs of the tall ladder. He brought down tennis shoes that had unevenly raised dots on the soles to dig into clay courts. Lauren and Lucas pretended to *swing* a tennis racket at the side, up and back, and *hit* the tennis ball forcefully over the net.

The salesperson suggested buying soccer shoes since the boys and girls in the neighborhood were beginning to form teams. The children *laced* up the black and white soccer shoes. They were called cleats because they had tiny sharp pointed rubber spikes to prevent players from slipping on the grass. "*Dig* your feet into the floor as you imagine yourself *dribbling* a soccer ball using the inside of each foot," said Lauren.

(cont.)

"May we try on football shoes?" asked Lucas. The salesperson nodded and said, "Yes," as he *climbed* seven rungs of the ladder. "*Run* backward for a long pass," yelled Lauren. "A little more, a little more, *stop* and *catch* the football." Both children *jumped* up and down because they had scored a touchdown!

"That was fun, but we can't play football all the time," said Lucas. "Please, can you show us a pair of hiking boots?" Lauren asked sweetly.

"I should wear hiking boots," thought the salesperson as he *climbed* six rungs of the ladder. Lauren and Lucas *pulled* on the heavily padded boots. The two children pretended to *throw* safety ropes and *climb* jagged rocks along wooded trails. "These shoes *make* me feel heavy," said Lauren, "I would like to try a pair of swim flippers." The salesperson watched the two children *sit* on the floor and quickly *flutter* their legs up and down to test the flippers.

Just as the two children were about to ask the salesperson to climb the ladder again, Lucas saw a soft pair of slippers with bunny ears and a fluffy tail. The two children eagerly *pointed to* the slippers. "Yes, yes, if that is what you want, but you must promise to *jump* like a bunny when you leave," said the salesperson as he *climbed* the ladder for the final time. The two children *scuffled* around the foot stool, *scampered* on their hands and feet, *sprang* upward high in the air, and finally pretended to *jump* like a bunny as they agreed to buy the warm and fuzzy slippers.

"We'll return tomorrow to buy sport shoes for school," said Lucas as the children *jumped* seven times to exit the store.

The salesperson *looked* at the large pile of opened boxes that needed to be replaced among the stacks of shoes. He *sat* on the floor and *leaned* backward supporting his tall body with his hands. "I wonder if those soft, fluffy slippers would fit me?" he asked with a long sigh.

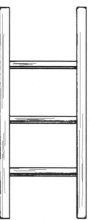

SPACE WORLD

One sunny afternoon, Jessie and Jeannie decided to take a trip to Space World. Their adventures began at the Moon Walk, where they were encouraged to *step* over five large moon craters. Real craters are made by stray pieces of rocks colliding with the moon. This exciting walk led the children to the Space Maze, where they *dashed* and *darted* through narrow pathways until they found a black hole to *crawl* through.

As the children *raised* their bodies, they saw a sign reading "Jupiter Jump." Here they were challenged to take eight *jumps* forward before moving on to Meteor Magic. Meteors or "shooting stars" burn up as they streak into the Earth's atmosphere. At the Meteor Magic station, the ground was very hot, so the two children *walked* on their *tiptoes* and then magically they *burst* into the Milky Way Mystery. Here the children *stretched* upward and tried to *touch* the bright stars. "I'm not leaving here," said Jessie, "Until I catch at least three shooting stars." Jeannie agreed, so the two children *raced* to *catch* one shooting star that was *rolling* along the ground. The second star *bounced* up and down three times before the children successfully controlled it, and the third star was *caught* at a high level over their heads.

In Planet Play, the children traveled through the solar system by *marching* in a circle around Mercury, performing *shaking* and *vibrating movements* around Venus, and *galloping* three times around Earth. They decided to *hop* on one foot around Mars, *jump* with two feet over Jupiter, *skip* around Saturn, and *leap* forward over Uranus. Jessie loved *swimming* around Neptune and *plodding* over Pluto. This playful pathway ended in the land of Space Invaders.

In this station, the children saw *wiggly* worms, *soaring* giant birds, and *creeping* animals with antennae. Feeling tired, the two children decided to take a relaxing ride in the Space Bubble. As their bubble *floated* freely in the air, they were almost asleep when they heard a giant pop! The Space Bubble had *burst* and they *fell* to the ground at the entrance of the Comet Ride. This station reminded the children of a giant roller coaster. They *grasped* the steel bar that was positioned in front of their bodies and they *zoomed* through space with the comet's glowing tail streaming behind them.

The last space station was the most challenging. It was called, "Save Our Planet." At this station, the children *collected* a bag filled with cans and bottles, *stacked* newspaper into piles, painted garbage cans, and learned about the importance of keeping the earth clean and safe. With this important message, Jessie and Jeannie *skipped* merrily home.

THE COMMUNITY HISTORY & SCIENCE MUSEUM

"Just think, all life began in the water!" Jason said, as he loudly *smacked* his lips and *stretched* upward *to set* the plastic glass container in the sink drain. "I wish I had been born when the giant dinosaurs roamed the earth."

"Not me," said Jackie. "Some of the first fish were sharks with pointed snouts, frightening jaws, and razor sharp teeth. I like my goldfish." The two children *grabbed* their Dinosaur backpacks, their Cave Dweller's lunch boxes, and their Prehistoric pencil cases, and *sprinted* to Dinosaur Kingdom, a favorite community attraction.

At the first learning center, a guide told the children a story about what it was like to live in prehistoric times. She began by asking the children what types of activities they enjoyed performing in the mountains. One child said, "I like to *climb* steep jagged rocks."

Another child said, "I like to *ski* down mountains, *dodging* trees and stumps." The guide told the children that mountains had *risen* upward from the ground. She also talked about the lakes that suddenly formed. Jason said, "I like to *swim*, *reel* in fish, and *ride* in speedboats at top speeds." The desert was another feature added to the Earth's surface. Julie volunteered to *jump* like a jackrabbit, *shake* like a rattlesnake's tail, and *howl* like a coyote. "The world must have been a fun place to live," said Jason.

"Oh no," said the guide. She told the children about sea creatures that had once lived in the ocean, and then *moved* to the land to lay and *bury* their eggs in the sand. They liked the heat and the bright desert sun. Over many years, this reptile family grew in strength and size and became known as the dinosaur, which means "terrible lizard."

The largest dinosaur was called the Brachiosaurus. It was tall enough *to stretch* over the top of a four-story building. It had strong front legs and its nose was a bump on the top of its head. Jason and Jackie were challenged to *move* like several large animals that still exist today. They pretended to *dive* through the water like the huge blue whale, which can weigh as much as thirty elephants. They *splashed* in make-believe water like hippopotami, and they *pounded* on their chests like gorillas.

"What animal exists today that has a bump on its body?" asked the guide. Jackie answered by *slumping* over and *walking* like the Arabian camel with a 300-pound load on its back.

At the second learning center, the children viewed a picture of the second largest dinosaur, which was named the Apatosaurus. This dinosaur was 80 feet long with legs as thick as tree trunks. It used to be called the Brontosaurus, which means "thunder reptile." The children were challenged to *walk* and *stomp* so that their footsteps sounded like thunder.

"The Apatosaurus liked to eat the leaves from the tallest trees," said the guide. "We have animals today that stand very tall. Who can *gallop, stop*, and *stretch* upward to *snatch* an imaginary apricot leaf like the 16-foot giraffe we see in the African Savanna? The giraffe *chomps* down on a branch of leaves, *pulls* its head back, and *strips* the leaves off the tree branch. Giraffes can eat more than 65 pounds of leaves in one day."

"Gee, that's how much I weigh," said Jackie.

In the third learning center, the children saw a movie about the Stegosaurus, which means "roofed reptile." This 30-foot-long creature had large bony plates on its back and tail. There were four sharp spikes at the end of his tail to swing out at other dinosaurs. The guide reminded the children of the porcupine. Porcupines are only the size of small dogs, but when one gets angry it *turns* its back on its attackers, *rattles* its quills, *grunts*, and *stamps* its feet. If you get too close, it may strike you with its tail, which is covered with sharp quills.

At learning center four, the children learned that some dinosaurs could fly, but they didn't have feathers. One of these was called the Rhamphorhynchus. It had skin that stretched from its front legs to its back claws. It *flapped* this skin to *glide* in the air and used its long tail to help it steer. Jason *jumped* up and said, "I can move like several large birds." So he *soared* like an eagle, *swooped* down to the water like a brown pelican spotting fish near the surface, and imagined he could *stretch* his arms to be like the nine-foot wings of the California condor.

At learning center five, the children marveled at the statue of the Styracosaurus. This dinosaur had huge horns on its head and a bony frill made of six sharp spikes around its neck. The frill was very heavy and caused it to *clomp* along slowly on four thick legs. Today's black rhinoceros has two large horns, and charges if it is attacked by a lion. Jason showed the group how to *scuff* at the ground and *charge* like a raging rhino.

Before moving on to learning center six, the guide asked the children, "Can you name three animals that have bills but don't fly?"

Julie said, "The ostrich stands eight feet tall and *runs* on its toes," as she *raced* quickly throughout the playing area.

"The king penguin *wobbles* as it *walks* on the ice," said Jason. Both children used their hands to show the *movement* of the peacock's bright blue fan tail as it *opens.*

"Good," said the guide, "You won't be surprised to see a cartoon program showing duck-billed dinosaurs." The children noticed that some of these dinosaurs had strange bones on top of their heads. Some were shaped like feathers, others looked like helmets, and some even looked like the blades of axes.

In learning center seven, the children were asked to move like the animals we see today that live on the land, and also swim in the water. Jason used his arms and *dragged* his body along the floor like a walrus. "Boy, I can see why the

(cont.)

walrus needs thick skin and strong arms and legs shaped like flippers. This is hard work," said Jason.

Jackie chose to *slip* and *slide* like the seal that can stay underwater for an hour before breathing.

The guide showed the children a large stuffed Archelon, and said, "This dinosaur looked like the turtle we see today, except that it was as large as a car!"

"Boy, you would need a large bowl for turtle soup!" said Jason. The two children pretended to have a shell and *moved* closely to the ground.

The next learning center contained a make-believe skeleton of the Tyrannosaurus Rex. The guide said, "This dinosaur was the largest of the meat-eating reptiles. It *walked* on two legs and could *lift* more than 400 pounds with its arms. It was the most feared by all the dinosaurs. It was feared like the lion, the king of beasts in the jungle." Jason pretended to *stalk* prey like a Tyrannosaurus Rex. "That's correct," said the guide.

"It's getting late, how many dinosaurs are there?" asked Jackie.

"Oh," said the guide, "There were more than 350 types of dinosaurs that ruled the earth for 165 million years."

"In that case, it might take at least three million years to visit all the learning centers!" said both children.

"No," said the guide, "Return tomorrow and we'll continue."

Jason and Jackie were leaving Dinosaur Kingdom when Jackie *spotted* a water fountain. "Do you want a refreshing drink of water, Jason?" she asked. "No thank you," he replied, as both children *leaped* over stone pebbles on their way home, "I think I'll switch to milk.

HOLIDAY MOUNTAIN

Chris and Carrie awoke on a cool winter morning in December feeling very happy. Their parents had given the children permission to visit Holiday Mountain. This was a special treat since Holiday Mountain reminded the children that Christmas would soon be here. The two *dressed* quickly as they *buttoned* their winter coats.

As they entered the tall white gates, both children were asked to join the Sugarplum Dancers. Together they *swayed* back and forth and *whirled* around to a lively beat. The song ended with partners *hooking* elbows and carefully *swinging* each other around in a circle. Feeling quite dizzy, the two children *wobbled* to Reindeer Ranch.

They admired the strong muscles in the reindeer's shoulders as they *snapped* the riding whip and yelled, "Giddy Up!" The reindeer proudly *pranced* and *galloped* as they *pulled* the red sleigh through the woods.

The sled approached the Gingerbread House. The children *made* footprints in the snow as they *trudged* to the house. They *stretched* upward to peek in the window. Inside they saw jars of long candy canes, tiny round gumdrops, and striped candy ribbon. Chris said, "We can make those shapes with our bodies!" He *curled* his arms to make the bend in the candy cane. Carrie *demonstrated* how to make a tiny ball shape, and both children made a *wavy* action with their arms to represent ribbon candy.

They were *giggling* loudly when Sally Snowflake, the owner of the house, surprised the two children. "I'm very special," she boastfully said. "Snowflakes are made from many creative shapes." She challenged the children to use their bodies and *make* four different snowflakes. Upon completion, Chris and Carrie thanked Sally as they *raced* to the Himalaya Mountain Ride.

The two children *climbed* upward to reach the peak of the steep mountain. Carrie was almost at the top when she *slipped* and began to *topple* downward. She *landed* in a large drift of soft snow. Chris came *running* with a shovel and began to *dig* in the snow. Soon, Carrie *arose, brushed* the snow from her coat, and *shook* her hat. "Well," she said, "I'm ready to take another ride." Chris laughed as the two quickly *climbed* to the top.

At the peak of the mountain was a large toboggan. They quickly *sat* down and *placed* their hands on the shoulders of the person sitting in the front. The giant toboggan *rocked* back and forth as it *slid* down the side of the mountain. The ride ended at the North Pole Playground.

The children *crawled* through a snow tunnel, *skated* around an icy pond, and *rolled a* giant snowball to build Frosty. The two children were

(cont.)

throwing snowballs at a target when a small elf yelled, "Don't miss the Jingle Bell Jamboree!" The two children took small, tiny *steps* behind the elf until they arrived at the Nutcracker Theater.

Both children were given jingle bells to *strap* onto their hands and feet. "Watch me," said Chris as he *shook* his arms and then his legs. Carrie showed how she could *flutter* her hands up to a high level and then all the way down to a low level. The two children *performed* three different Jingle Bell dances by *shaking, spinning,* and *stretching* in different directions, before returning the bells to the elf.

They were *buttoning* their coats and *pulling* on their boots to walk home when Carrie said, "Wait, I still hear bells." Both children slowly *looked* upward into the sky.

From a distance they could hear the sound of bells and someone laughing, "Ho, Ho, Ho." The two children *winked* and *laughed* as they *strolled* through the tall white gates.

HALLOWEEN

Primary Learning Objective: The children will use their bodies and make-believe they are objects associated with Halloween.

Materials or Equipment: None

Formation: Children are in their personal spaces.

Individual or Partner Learning Experience:
The teacher presents the following:

1. Imagine you are wearing a Halloween mask. Show me what it looks like.

2. Can you *make* a round pumpkin shape with your arms? Who can *add* a silly face to their Jack-O-Lantern?

3. Is it possible to *drift* through the air like a ghost?

4. *Hold* your broomstick handle and *fly* through the air like a witch.

5. How would you *stretch* and *arch* your body like a black cat?

6. Find a way to *move* on your hands and feet like a spider.

7. *Walk* with stiff legs like Frankenstein.

8. *Shake* your bony arms and legs as you *move* like a skeleton.

9. Pretend to *flap* your wings and *glide* like a bat.

10. Act as if you are a *creeping, crawling,* long creature.

11. *Swing* your long tail, roar, and *breathe* fire as you *stomp* loudly like a dragon.

12. Show me how you can *walk* like black cats on your tiptoes along a narrow fence.

13. How would you *move* if one partner pretended to be a broom and the other pretended to be a witch?

14. Spiders have many legs. Can you and a partner *move* together like a spider?

15. Bats have two wings. *Stand* beside a partner and *place* your inside arms around each other's shoulders. *Fly* like a bat.

16. *Skip* along with your friend and make-believe you are *carrying* a large Halloween bag.

Whole-Group Learning Experience:
FOUR-PERSON MONSTER: Challenge the children to create a four-person monster.

HAUNTED HOUSE: Divide the children into two groups. One group constructs the walls of a house by forming two side-by-side lines facing each other. The second group of children make-believe they are trick or treaters and merrily skip throughout the playing area. At some point, the teacher indicates that it is nightfall. At this point, the walls of the house can reach out, move, and shake in their personal spaces to scare the children. Walls should not grab at the trick or treaters. Exchange roles.

Creative Closure:

1. Name three things you should do to be safe on Halloween.

2. Use your imagination to show me how a spook moves through a haunted house.

WINTER HOLIDAYS

Primary Learning Objective: The children will be actively engaged in a variety of winter holiday movements.

Materials or Equipment: None

Formation: Children are in their personal spaces.

Individual or Partner Learning Experience:
The teacher presents the following:

1. Can you *walk* like a gingerbread boy or girl with your arms *outstretched*?

2. Show me how Rudolph the reindeer *gallops* and *flies* through the air.

3. *Sway* back and forth like a Christmas bell. Say "ding-dong."

4. *Make* the shape of a candy cane at a low level.

5. Show me a long and thin chimney shape. *Wiggle* your fingers like smoke rising from the chimney.

6. Is it possible to let your body *hang* downward like a Christmas sock? Now slowly *stretch* your arms wide as the sock is filled.

7. Can you *shape* your body to look like a Christmas or Chanukah present? Is it possible to *bend* your bodies to create a large gift box bow?

8. March like a tin soldier throughout general space.

9. Find the best way to *form* your body into a tiny, round Christmas bulb.

10. Who can *create* a five pointed star with his or her body? Which body parts make the points of the star?

11. Use your bodies to *make* the shape of a large round wreath.

12. Show me how a dreidel *spins*.

Whole-Group Learning Experience:
IGLOOS: Explain to the children that they can make an igloo by having some children stand and form the large dome, while other children kneel on their knees to make the tunnel entrance.

SNOWPERSON: Ask the children how many bodies are needed to make a snow-person and to demonstrate.

TOBOGGAN: Have the children position their bodies as if they were riding a long toboggan.

A SNOWFLAKE: Invite the children to create a giant snowflake by having everyone's body make a wide shape while becoming connected.

SANTA'S SLED: Ask the children to demonstrate what Santa's sled might look like. Some children will be reindeer standing side-by-side, others will make a box shape for the sled, and one child will be a make-believe Santa Claus standing at the end of the sled.

STRING OF LIGHTS: Encourage the children to find the best way to make a long string of Christmas lights.

NOEL: The word Noel means Christmas. Challenge the children to combine their bodies to spell the word Noel?

THE MENORAH: Prompt the children to create a menorah with nine children's bodies standing like candles. Eight candles represent the eight days of Chanukah, and the ninth candle is the Shamos or leader and stands taller than the other candles. The Shamos candle lights the others. As the candles are lit, the flames flicker and flutter, causing the candles to melt.

Creative Closure:

1. Can you think of an object that is red or green?

2. During winter holidays, we sometimes see two different types of angels. Show me how you can lie down at a low level and move your arms and legs to create snow angels. Now, place your hands on your hips and fly throughout the playing area.

CHAPTER 5

Developing the Child's Appreciation
of Living Creatures and the Environment

Developing the Child's Appreciation of Living Creatures and the Environment

The young child's first experiences with his or her surroundings begins within the home and later extends throughout the community (see Chapter 4). As children gain confidence in the home environment, they develop greater curiosity about their school surroundings and beyond. Children become fascinated with living creatures that are not common to their home. They soon learn that these creatures can be classified according to where they most often live. They also find enjoyment in imitating the movements, characteristics, and behaviors of specific animals, while gaining an appreciation for the differing patterns and movement skills needed to "become" the animal. Teachers can enhance this experience by making comparisons between the child's human body and that of other living creatures, while also recognizing physical differences among other groups such as animals, birds, fish, and insects. Therefore, the first part of this chapter is designed to increase the child's appreciation for living creatures, and to satisfy the child's natural curiosity of the unknown or little known, through moderate and vigorous movement-based learning experiences.

 For example, a photograph of a snail and a turtle can be shown during an individual and partner learning experience with the teacher asking the children, "Can you curl your body into the shape of a snail's shell?" followed by challenging partners to form a make-believe turtle shell. This is possible when one child lies on the floor/ground on his or her stomach. The other partner stretches over the first partner's body, with hands touching the floor, to form the shell. Together, children can move slowly.

In another example, the whole-group learning experience includes children identifying living creatures that live in caves (e.g., bear, mountain lion, bat, spider, snake). The children are divided into two groups. One group represents animals and living creatures that can be found in caves. In the second group, each child has a partner and together they form a cave by facing each other and stretching arms upward while touching hands. The first group enacts animal movements and sounds while moving in and out of caves. Children then exchange roles.

The second part of this chapter is aimed at having the child gain a greater awareness of differing environments such as the seashore, forest, the ocean, and the actions of people who are involved in helping preserve our natural world, and descriptive roles of environmental professionals.

Animal Fun Facts

Elephants are the only animals that can't jump.
The African elephant has ears that can grow to four feet wide.
The giraffe is the tallest animal in the world.
All polar bears are left-handed.
Tigers have striped skin, not just striped fur.

Birds Fun Facts

There are more chickens than people in the world.
A duck's quack doesn't echo, and no one knows why.
The hummingbird can fly straight up like a helicopter.
The North American loon can dive 160 feet deep.
The Bar-headed goose flies over 25,000 miles high into the sky.

Fish Fun Facts

The shark is the only fish that can blink with both eyes.
A goldfish has a memory span of three seconds.
The giant squid has the largest eyes in the world.
Most fish that live in water where sunlight cannot reach (i.e., at least 600 feet deep)
   have lantern organs that flash on and off in the dark.
The flounder is a flat fish with two eyes on one side of its body and changes its
   skin color to hide from its enemies.

Insects Fun Facts

A dragonfly, the fastest flying insect, can fly 60 miles an hour.
Butterflies taste with their feet.
An ant can lift 50 times its body weight.
A flea can broad jump approximately 13 inches.
All insects have six legs.

INSECT MOVEMENTS

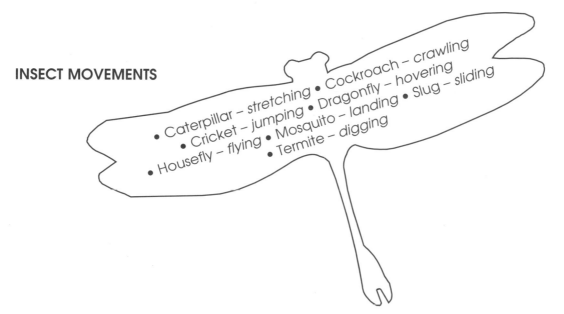

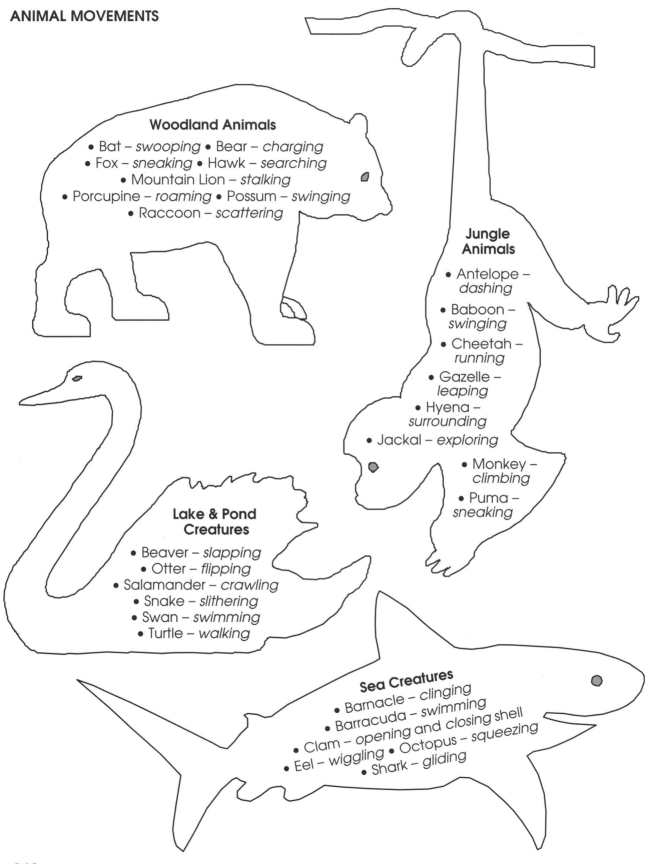

Woodland Animals
- Bat – *swooping* • Bear – *charging*
- Fox – *sneaking* • Hawk – *searching*
- Mountain Lion – *stalking*
- Porcupine – *roaming* • Possum – *swinging*
- Raccoon – *scattering*

Jungle Animals
- Antelope – *dashing*
- Baboon – *swinging*
- Cheetah – *running*
- Gazelle – *leaping*
- Hyena – *surrounding*
- Jackal – *exploring*
- Monkey – *climbing*
- Puma – *sneaking*

Lake & Pond Creatures
- Beaver – *slapping*
- Otter – *flipping*
- Salamander – *crawling*
- Snake – *slithering*
- Swan – *swimming*
- Turtle – *walking*

Sea Creatures
- Barnacle – *clinging*
- Barracuda – *swimming*
- Clam – *opening and closing shell* • Octopus – *squeezing*
- Eel – *wiggling* • Shark – *gliding*

ANIMALS OF THE WORLD

Primary Learning Objective: The children will learn how animals from different regions move and demonstrate these movements.

Materials or Equipment: None

Formation: Children are in their personal spaces.

Individual or Partner Learning Experience:
The teacher presents the following:

1. We can pretend to visit the zoo to learn about different animals. African elephants can grow to be 10 feet tall at the shoulders. They have big ears and a nose called a trunk. They use their trunks for tearing off leaves and clumps of grass to eat, smelling, and squirting water into their mouths. Show me how you can *bend* forward and use your arms to make a trunk that is low to the ground. Can you *swing* your trunk from side to side as you *move* like a heavy elephant?

2. The giraffe can grow to be 19 feet tall. They get most of their food and water from leaves high in the trees, and can go a month without water. *Grasp* your hands together and *stretch* them upward like the long neck of a giraffe. *Gallop* forward.

3. Is it possible to *swing* your arms low to the ground, and to the side like a gorilla?

4. The fastest land animal is the cheetah. It can *run* up to 65 miles an hour. Show me how you can run fast by *pumping* your arms at the side of your body and *sprinting* forward.

5. Some African frogs can jump 10 feet. See if you can *stoop* low to the ground and *spring* forward, using the muscles in your legs.

(cont.)

6. Kangaroos live in Australia and use their powerful legs to jump as far as 40 feet and as high as 10 feet. *Tuck* your hands to the side of your chest and see how far you can *jump* forward from a standing position.

7. Alligators have short arms and legs and a very long body. You can move like an alligator by *lying* on the floor and *moving* your hand and foot on one side of your body and then the other hand and foot. *Bend* your legs and elbows as you move.

8. The pink flamingo is a large, web-footed bird with very long and slender legs and neck. This bird loves to wade in water. Try to *balance* on one foot like the pink flamingo.

9. The bear is a heavy animal with thick fur and sharp claws. The bear shifts its body from side to side to move forward. Who can *bend* forward and *touch* the ground with both hands and feet? Now *move* a front and a back paw on the same side of your body. *Shift* to the other front and back paw while you *move* and growl.

10. The seal is a flesh-eating sea animal and has large flippers. Its long body is covered with thick fur or bristle. The seal uses its front flippers and drags its tail to move along the ice. Is it possible to *move* forward by only *using* your hands and *dragging* your feet?

Whole-Group Learning Experience:
MONKEYS ON THE MOVE: Explain to the children that monkeys are active animals that use their strong arms to move from vines to tree branches. Challenge the children to use their bodies to make-believe they are a group of monkeys swinging playfully. One half of the class uses their arms to form vines or tree branches. The remaining children are monkeys and make-believe they are swinging from branch to branch by moving under the branches (i.e., arms) of the trees. Ask the "monkeys" to demonstrate how they can swing on every branch. Exchange roles.

Creative Closure:

1. Who can demonstrate the movements and sounds of their favorite animal?

2. If you could travel anywhere in the world, what animal would you like to see living in its natural habitat? Can you show me how this animal moves?

JUNGLE GYMNASTICS

Primary Learning Objective: The children will identify and perform the action words of a simple animal rhyme.

Materials or Equipment: Ribbons, scarves, or cloths that are 18 inches long

Formation: Children are in their personal spaces.

Individual or Partner Learning Experience:
The teacher presents the following:

1. Have you ever heard of Jungle Gymnastics?
   Is it possible to act out the movements in the following rhyme?

   Imagine a riverboat,
   Floating down the Nile.
   Keep alert and you will see
   A *snapping* crocodile.

   In tropical rain forests,
   With funny looking trees,
   There are *crawly* bugs, and *slithering* snakes,
   Colorful birds and *swinging* chimpanzees.

   Now, let's change this rhyme a bit,
   So you'll get exercise.
   Forget that you are a child and
   Try an animal disguise.

   First, *stand* and *hold* your arms out,
   And use your arms to *fly.*
   You're a colorful, yakking bird,
   Stretching upward to the sky.

   Now, *bend* your legs a little,
   And *put* your hands down on the floor.
   Stretch your body forward,
   And *make* a lion's roar!

   If we were lions we could *stride* or *strut* as we walk,
   Or *sneak* about or pretend to *stalk.*
   We could *shuffle* along on our paws or feet,
   Make loud roaring sounds. Isn't that neat!

2. With a partner, create a jungle animal complete with sounds (e.g., gorilla, monkey, elephant, cheetah, rhinoceros).

Whole-Group Learning Experience:
MONKEYS AND GORILLAS: Ask the children to identify how a monkey is different from a gorilla (i.e., monkeys have tails). Divide the children into two groups. One group are monkeys. Place a strip of ribbon or cloth in their waistbands so that at least six inches is showing. The second group are gorillas and scatter throughout the "jungle." In the middle of the "jungle" is a clearly marked circular area designated as the monkey tree.

(cont.)

On the teacher's signal, the monkeys leave the tree to search for imaginary bananas while gorillas try to snatch a tail. Whenever a gorilla is successful, he or she retreats to the monkey tree where he or she tucks in the "tail" and becomes a monkey. The child whose tail was pulled now becomes a gorilla. However, gorillas cannot take away a monkey's tail while the monkey is in the tree.

All monkeys leaving the tree have five free seconds in which their tails cannot be taken. This keeps gorillas away from the tree. Children can perform a variety of movement patterns while adding monkey and gorilla sounds and actions. Remind the children that the monkey tree is only used to adjust tails and is not a resting area.

Creative Closure:

1. Who can name five additional jungle animals?

2. Can someone show us how one of those animals move, and we will copy you.

SEA CREATURES

Primary Learning Objective: The children will demonstrate basic movement skills while identifying sea creatures and differentiating between their movement patterns.

Materials or Equipment: None

Formation: Children are in their personal spaces.

Individual or Partner Learning Experience:
The teacher presents the following:

1. Sea creatures can live in warm tropical waters and in cold, dark waters. Fish are sea creatures and they have a backbone. Jellyfish do not have a backbone or a skeleton. Let's *jump* into the water and use our arms to *float* like jellyfish.

2. The flying fish swims to the surface and leaps out of the water. Its fins are spread out to help it glide through the air. Can you *spread* your fins and *move* like the flying fish?

3. The sea horse has a horse-like head, a hard shell like an insect, and a pouch like a kangaroo. The sea horse swims by wiggling its back fin and moves up and down almost like a horse on a merry-go-round. Who can *swim* like a sea horse?

4. Puffer fish and porcupine fish make themselves swell up like a balloon so that larger fish have problems swallowing them. Try to make your body *puff* up to a larger shape.

5. The octopus has eight arms, with suckers along the bottoms of its arms for gripping. Demonstrate how an octopus might *move* along the ocean floor.

6. There are over 250 types of sharks. The tiger, great white, and hammerhead sharks are the most well-known "killer" sharks. They are hunters with very large teeth. Find a way to *show* your large teeth while *pretending* to hunt for prey.

8. The moray eel looks like a snake but is a fish. Show me how you would *hide* in a hole and *wiggle* out at night to hunt for sea creatures.

Whole-Group Learning Experience:
THE BIG SWIM: Organize the children in a side-by-side line on one end line, facing the opposite end of the playing area. Designate one child to be the King or Queen of the Sea, and have that child stand in the center of the playing area. The two end lines are clearly marked. Individual children choose a specific sea creature to imitate. When the King or Queen of the Sea says, "Swim, Swim, Swim," the children move like their selected sea creature to the other end of the playing area.

If a child is tagged in the center of the playing area, that child joins the King or Queen of the Sea. The King or Queen of the Sea can try to trick the children by using phrases like "Swim Flipper, Swim." The last three or four remaining sea creatures are declared "Star Fish," and become the next Kings or Queens of the Sea. Always reinforce the need to avoid stepping on another child's hands, especially those of children choosing to be slithering sea creatures.

Creative Closure:

1. As a human, what sea creature is easiest for you to imitate its movements? Why?

2. Let's combine our bodies to create a giant whale shape.

LOBSTER MOVEMENTS

Primary Learning Objective: The child will show an appreciation for the unique movements of a crustacean while coordinating stepping actions with other children.

Materials or Equipment: None

Formation: Children are in their personal spaces.

Individual or Partner Learning Experience:
The teacher presents the following:

1. Lobsters, crabs, and shrimp are sea creatures having five pairs of jointed legs. A pair of something means two. How many pairs of body parts do we have (e.g., two legs, eyes, ears, hands, arms, knees, elbows, and ankles)?

2. Can you *squeeze* your two elbows together? *Twirl* your wrists? *Dangle* your arms down by your toes?

3. Who can *blink* both eyes at the same time? *Tap* your ears?

4. Is it possible to *shake* your knees? Now *shake* your hands.

5. Find a way to *move* both ankles at the same time.

Whole-Group Learning Experience:
LOBSTERS ON THE MOVE: Remind the children that lobsters have five pairs of jointed legs. Therefore, they need five pairs of legs or five bodies to form one lobster. Ask the children to form groups of five. Each group of five quickly places their hands on the shoulders of the child in front. The child at the front of each group uses his or her arms to form the lobster's claws.

Introduce the fact that lobsters can move backward. Standing still, have the children stomp three times on one side of the body and then stomp three times on the other side. The group as a whole then shuffles backward three steps. For a greater challenge, designate specific locations within the playing area for each group to move through (e.g., a make-believe rocky beach, dune area, lagoon, sandy beach, or sand bar).

Creative Closure:

1. Who can tell me what part of a lobster is used to help the sea creature swim backwards (the tail)?

2. Can you think of other sea life that we can create with our bodies? Show me.

BIRDS OF A FEATHER

Primary Learning Objective: The children will explore unique ways birds move.

Materials or Equipment: None

Formation: Children are in their personal spaces.

Individual or Partner Learning Experience:
The teacher presents the following:

1. All birds have wings but some birds cannot fly.
   Penguins have wings and *waddle* when they walk. See if you can *waddle* like a penguin.

2. The ostrich cannot fly but is the fastest running bird in the world. When it runs 40 miles per hour, its wings are held straight out to the sides for balance. Try to *move* like an ostrich. Can you demonstrate how an ostrich *squats* down and *stretches* its long neck along the ground to *hide* from enemies?

3. Some birds have flaps of skin between their toes that act as small paddles to move quickly through the water. Lying on your back with your legs raised in the air, discover how a duck's feet would *move* underwater.

4. The male peacock spreads its large tail to attract the attention of female birds. The male turkey also spreads his tail and puffs his body to look much bigger and more colorful. Show me how you can *strut* about like a peacock or turkey, showing off your colorful tails.

5. Woodpeckers use their four sharp, clawed toes to hop up the sides of trees. Pretend you are a woodpecker and take small *hops*.

Whole-Group Learning Experience:
DUCKS IN A ROW: Explain to the children that when the mother duck leads her ducklings to the pond for a swim, all the ducklings waddle in a single-file line behind her. The children are divided into four groups. One child in each group is the mother duck, and the other children are the ducklings. The children will imitate bird movements while waddling throughout the playing area following the mother duck to the water.

MIGRATION: Tell the children that in the fall, many birds fly in groups, called flocks, to relocate to a warmer climate. Many birds fly in a "V" formation. Ask the children to make a fist and extend the index and middle fingers to form a "V" shape. When the lead bird is tired, that bird drops back to the end of a line and another bird takes the lead. Divide the children into four groups. Designate one child in each group to be the lead duck. The teacher can announce, "Change" and the leader will fall back while another goose takes the lead.

Creative Closure:

1. Do all birds move in the same way?

2. Can you think of another bird we did not talk about today and how it moves? Show me.

PENGUINS

Primary Learning Objective: The children will exhibit responsible and personal behavior while participating in an action rhyme.

Materials or Equipment: Floor markers

Formation: Children are in their personal spaces.

Individual or Partner Learning Experience:
The teacher presents the following:

1. The penguin has a long, pointed beak.
   What body part do we have that is like the penguin's beak? Can you *point* to it?

2. The penguin's wings are at the sides of the body. Try to *flap* the two body parts we have at the sides of our body.

3. Let's pretend you are a community of penguins waddling across the ice. See if you can *stand* very tall like the King Penguins who live in the Antarctic, where it is very cold.

4. Who can keep their legs very *stiff* and take a tiny *step* forward with one leg? Now take a tiny *step* forward with the other leg.

5. Penguins waddle along the ice by shifting one side of the body at a time. Show me how you can keep your arms at the sides of the body while you *waddle?*

6. Imagine you are a penguin. Is it possible to act out the movements in the following rhyme?

   Penguins *waddling* on the ice,
   They think the ice is nice
   But the sunshine in the day,
   Starts to *melt* the ice away.

   Then, the ice becomes much too small,
   Much too small to hold them all.
   So they *slide* and *slide* and *leap*,
   They all *splash* into the deep.

   And they *swim* away a little faster,
   Until they all will meet once more,
   On a cold and icy shore.

7. Facing a partner, one child *imitates* penguin movements, and the other child *mirrors* those movements. Exchange roles.

Whole-Group Learning Experience:
A PENGUIN PARADE: Ask the children to select a partner with one child standing behind the other. The first child is the lead penguin and waddles throughout the playing area in his or her choice of selected pathways. The second child follows the first child. Exchange roles. The teacher then designates one child to become the lead penguin while all of the other children form a single-file line behind the first penguin. All of the children waddle and follow the first penguin's pathways to create a parade of penguins.

A GIANT ICEBERG: Challenge the children to waddle throughout the playing area, which is an imaginary iceberg, without touching another child's body. At the teacher's signal, penguins freeze (i.e., stop moving).

Markers are placed on the floor to create a smaller, melting iceberg. The activity continues until the iceberg becomes too small for the penguins. The children are encouraged to jump off the iceberg into imaginary water. They use their arms as fins to swim to the safety of another iceberg, another designated area.

Creative Closure:

1. What body parts did you use to move like the penguin?

2. Can you think of another animal who lives where there is ice and snow? Let's try to imitate those animal movements.

THE EAGLE AND THE CHICKEN

Primary Learning Objective: The child will differentiate between the movements of two birds and find enjoyment in being expressive.

Materials or Equipment: None

Formation: Children are in their personal spaces.

Individual or Partner Learning Experience:
The teacher presents the following:

1. Can you tell me the differences between an eagle and a chicken?

2. Let's perform the actions in the following movement narrative:

> A young eaglet became lost in the barnyard of a chicken farm.
> Not knowing any better, it thought that it must be a chicken.
> So, it did all the things it saw the chickens do.
>
> They *scratch* (children *scratch* the ground with toes of one foot, three times)
> And *peck* (children *make* pecking motions with their heads, three times)
> And *cluck* (children *click* their tongues as they tip their heads from side to side three times)
> And *squawk* (children *squawk* three times)
> And occasionally *cock-a-doodle-doo* too (children *crow* cock-a-doodle-doo three times)!
>
> The eagle *grew* bigger and bigger (children *puff* out their chests).
> It *grew* bigger than the chickens (children *stretch* outward).
> It *grew* bigger than the rooster (children *reach* upward).
> It could *run* faster than they could (children *run* in place).
> And *jump* higher than they could (children *jump* up).
>
> The eagle became very uncomfortable. It needed more space to run and jump.
>
> The chickens were very happy doing all the things that chickens do.
> They *scratched* (children *scratch* the ground with toes of one foot, three times)
> And *pecked* (children *make* pecking motions with their heads, three times)
> And *clucked* (children *click* their tongues as they tip their heads from side to side three times)
> And *squawked* (children *squawk* three times)
> And occasionally *crowed* cock-a doodle-doo too (children *crow* cock-a-doodle-doo three times)!
>
> One day, the eagle *looked* up and *saw* an eagle flying in the sky. It said, "That is a big bird! It's as big as I am. I wonder if I could fly like that."
>
> So, it *ran* as fast as it could (children *run* in place)
> And it *flapped* its wings as hard as it could (children *flap* their arms)
> And it *jumped* as high as it could (children *jump* up)
> But it could not fly. It was not strong enough.
>
> One day it *ran* as fast as it could (children *run* in place)
> And it *flapped* its wings as hard as it could (children *flap* their arms)
> And it *jumped* as high as it could (children *jump* up)

And it *flew* up into the air.
It *flew* higher than the barn.
It *flew* higher than the treetops.
It said, "It's big out here! I want to see all of it!"

It *flew* and it *flew* until it came to the top of the highest mountain.
There it *saw* lots of eagles.
Other eagles joined him and began to do all the things that eagles do.

They *fly* (children *run* flapping their arms)
And *glide* (children *stretch* their arms out straight as they run)
And *swoop* (children *bend* and *move* their knees and bodies as though swooping down)
And *soar* (children *raise* up on their toes and *reach* their arms straight up)
And one particular eagle, when no one is looking,
Will occasionally *cock-a-doodle-doo* (children *crow* cock-a-doodle-doo three times).

Whole-Group Learning Experience:

EAGLE'S NEST: Organize the children into three groups. One group performs the movements of an eagle. The second group creates an eagle's nest, or aerie, which can be as large as nine feet in diameter. The third group are fish, an eagle's favorite food. On the teacher's signal, the eagles will soar throughout the playing area, tagging as many fish as possible. When a fish is tagged, he or she is escorted to the nest, by the eagle that tagged him or her. After all the fish are caught, all three groups exchange roles.

Creative Closure:

1. The eagle is able to see both forward and to the side at the same time. Who can think of a special ability that humans have?

2. Using your arms as wings, how many ways can you soar in the air?

GIANT SPIDER WEB

Primary Learning Objective: The child will differentiate between wide and narrow shapes in a vigorous chase and flee activity.

Materials or Equipment: None

Formation: Children are in their personal spaces.

Individual or Partner Learning Experience:
The teacher presents the following:

1. How would you *stretch* your body into a wide shape? The distance between one hand and the other hand is very wide. When we talk about objects being very wide, we are describing the distance of the object from one side to the other.

2. Show me a wide shape at a low level.

3. Can you *make* a thin, narrow shape at a low level?

4. Is it possible to *combine* your body with a partner's body and *make* a wide shape at a high level? Try this at a low level.

5. How many different wide shapes can you and your partner *create* at a low level?

Whole-Group Learning Experience:
A SPIDER WEB: Assign two children to be the chasers or "spiders." The remainder of the children are "flies" and flee from the two spiders. Explain that as each child is tagged, he or she moves to a designated space in "the spider's den" (i.e., the playing area) and makes a wide shape on the floor.

Other children who are tagged join the first child, and combine their wide body shapes to form one giant spider web.

Encourage the children to connect their bodies in a variety of positions (e.g., head to head, foot to knee, elbow to hand). After all "flies" are tagged, the two spiders are permitted to carefully walk through the web by stepping into the spaces that appear between the children's body parts. Select new spiders each time the Spider Web activity is played.

Using a limited play space, children can make wide shapes while at a high level (e.g., standing). The spiders can move through the spider web represented by the children who are connected at medium and high levels.

Creative Closure:

1. Can you show me a wide shape using only your legs? Why was it important to form a wide body shape, and not a narrow shape, when you are forming the spider web?

2. How much floor space would be covered if the flies formed narrow shapes instead of wide shapes? How quickly can you create a giant spider web by using only narrow shapes?

BIG BUGS AND INSECTS

Primary Learning Objective: The children will make comparisons and demonstrate relationships between the human body and insect body.

Materials or Equipment: None

Formation: Children are in their personal spaces.

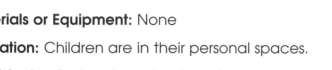

Individual or Partner Learning Experience:
The teacher presents the following:

1. Can you name things that move by creeping, squirming, wiggling, or crawling? There are millions of insects, and it would be impossible to name them all. We can participate in a movement activity to learn more about insects. For example, crickets hear with their legs. *Touch* the body part we use to hear sounds. Show me ways we *use* our legs.

2. Insects have feelers called antennae. They can smell food with their antennae. *Tap* the body part we use to smell foods. How do you *move* when you smell cookies in the oven?

3. Insects breathe through holes in their sides. Take a deep breath and *point* to the body parts we use for breathing. Can you *run* in your personal space until you are breathing very quickly?

4. The hair on an insect's body is used to taste and feel things. *Wiggle* the body part we use to taste foods and *shake* the body parts we use to feel objects.

5. Termites make nests in the soil. These nests have many tunnels. Can you *make* your body into a tunnel shape?

6. Pretend you are a firefly hiding in the daylight. Make-believe it is very dark and *use* your light to find other fireflies.

Whole-Group Learning Experience:
A DRAGONFLY: Explain to the children that they can combine their bodies to form large bugs and insects. The dragonfly is a swift-flying, graceful insect that patrols the edges of streams and ponds. It is recognized by its jeweled eyes that cover more than half of its head. The dragonfly has two pairs of transparent wings, six legs, and a long slender body. It also has two sets of jaws, with piercing teeth to eat mosquitoes and blackflies. Dragonflies are created by having groups of three children form a single-file line. The first two children in line extend their arms at the side of the body to represent the dragonfly's wings. The third child reaches over the second child to the shoulders of the first child. The three children coordinate leg movements to move forward.

A TARANTULA: The tarantula spider lives on the ground where it digs deep burrows. It is known for its hairy body, painful bite, and three-inch body with five-inch legs. Like other spiders, the tarantula has four pairs of legs. To create a make-believe tarantula, groups of four children huddle closely together with their arms on each other's shoulders. Each group moves throughout the playing area by coordinating leg movements and keeping their heads close together to represent the tarantula's body.

(cont.)

A CENTIPEDE: The centipede is a worm-like insect with one head, three mouths, one pair of antennae, two front claws, and a long, segmented body that can grow to 12 inches in length. By day, they live under rocks or in the bark of trees. Most types of centipedes have 10 pairs of legs, although some families may have as many as 177 legs. To form a centipede, groups of five children form a single-file line. Each child curls his or her body slightly forward to grasp the thighs of the child standing in front. The group slowly moves forward. If a mat or floor covering is available, the children can form a single-file line, kneel downward, and grasp the ankles of the child in front. In this position, the groups move forward in a slow shuffling motion.

ARMY ANTS: Army ants are always moving and searching for food. In areas where it is hot, they march in large groups. Encourage the children to join others to march throughout the playing area.

Creative Closure:

1. Today you learned about many different types of insects and how they move. Who can recall three facts we learned today?

2. Is it possible to form groups of three and create an imaginary insect?

THE BUMBLEBEE'S BODY

Primary Learning Objective: The child will make comparisons between his or her own body parts and a bee's anatomy while participating in a variety of movement activities.

Materials or Equipment: Six or seven beanbags or similar small objects that can be gripped, lively background music

Formation: Children are in their personal spaces.

Individual or Partner Learning Experience:
The teacher presents the following:

1. We can learn how the bumblebee's body is like or unlike our own body. Bumblebees have two sets of eyes on each side of their head. *Point* to the location of your eyes. How many sets of eyes do you have (one set)?

2. Bees hear through antennae. *Touch* the body parts we use to hear sounds. The bee's stinger projects from its abdomen. Can you *rub* your abdomen?

3. The bee's skeleton is on the outside of its body. Our skeleton is on the inside of the body. Find a way to *stretch* your fingers to make your hand very wide, and *point* to a bone inside your hand.

4. People talk or communicate through their mouths or with their hands. Bees communicate by dancing. "The Tail Wagging Dance," which looks like a wiggle, tells other bees where to find food. *Show* me what that dance might look like.

5. We use our legs to walk. Bees use their wings to fly. The buzzing sound is made from the rapid movement of the wings. Can you *place* two closed fists in front of your chest to form the wings of the bee? Who can *make* the movement and the buzzing sound of the bee?

Whole-Group Learning Experience:
THE BEE'S SONNET: Organize the children into two groups. One half of the children pretend to be flowers scattered throughout the playing area. The remainder of the children assume the role of bees and fly to each flower as lively music plays. Exchange roles.

THE BALANCING BEE: The children are encouraged to move at different levels throughout the playing area. At some point, the children are challenged to hover (i.e., freeze) and balance on one foot.

THE FLIGHT OF THE BUMBLEBEE: The children are encouraged to demonstrate the action of the bee, and "bee quick" or "bee fast" while moving throughout the playing area.

COLLECTING POLLEN: Divide the children into two groups. Partners in the first group join hands and squat down. With their arms, they form a large round circle, representing the opening to a beehive. The remaining children display the actions and sounds of the bees as they fly about collecting pollen (i.e., beanbags or other small objects). The bees take the pollen to the beehive. The children exchange roles after the pollen is collected.

Creative Closure:
1. What body parts can we exercise in order to move more quickly (legs)? Can you exercise your legs?

2. The bee needs to move its wings very quickly to keep its body in the air. Show me how quickly you are able to move your arms.

BUTTERFLIES

Primary Learning Objective: The children will discover the four phases of the life cycle of the butterfly and experience movements related to the butterfly.

Materials or Equipment: Two pieces of crepe paper per child, pictures of flowers displayed throughout the playing area

Formation: Children are scattered throughout the playing area.

Individual and Partner Learning Experience:
The teacher presents the following:

1. The word butterfly comes from the English word "buterfleoge," which means butter and flying creature. The butterfly goes through four stages of development. The first stage is the egg. Eggs are very tiny and can be round, oval, cylindrical, or other shapes. Can you *curl* your body into the shape of a butterfly egg?

2. Inside each egg is a caterpillar. The caterpillar has 16 legs, a hairy back, and very small eyes and mouth. Show me how you *wiggle* your body like the soft caterpillar.

3. The caterpillar pushes out of the egg and immediately begins to eat, growing very rapidly. This is the larval stage. The caterpillar's main activity is eating, and as it grows, it becomes too large for its skin. The caterpillar *sheds* its outer skin called the exoskeleton. Newly formed skin is developed. Can you show me how the caterpillar *pushes* out of its egg, *eats,* and then *sheds* its skin?

4. The third stage of the development of the butterfly is the pupa stage. When the caterpillar becomes an adult, usually after two weeks, it finds a high twig or leaf, hangs on, usually upside down, and covers its body with a sticky liquid. This shiny liquid hardens to become a golden colored shell. *Demonstrate* the caterpillar in this pupa stage by *shaping* your body into the letter "J." This is the shape the chrysalis looks like when suspended from the twig or leaf.

5. The butterfly is now ready to emerge from the pupa. Its wings are damp and crinkled. Try to free yourself from your chrysalis and show how you practice *moving* your wings until they unfold and are ready for flight.

Whole-Group Learning Experience:

FLIGHT OF THE BUTTERFLY: Explain to the children that butterflies flutter and fly to flowers, using their proboscis, a long sucking tube, to suck nectar and other liquids. Provide each child with two streamers to flutter and fly throughout the playing area. Ask the children to fly to flowers displayed on walls.

HIDE BUTTERFLY HIDE: Tell the children that butterflies have enemies, including birds and other insects. Many butterflies protect themselves by blending into the colors of their surroundings. Give each child two streamers. Select two children to be birds who will fly throughout the playing area. The other children are butterflies who flutter and fly. When the butterfly feels that it will be touched (i.e., captured) by a bird, the butterfly freezes (i.e., blends into its surroundings). If the butterfly is caught, it exchanges its wings (i.e., colored streamers) with the bird and flies away.

Creative Closure:

1. Why do you think people enjoy watching butterflies?

2. What happens to the wings of the butterfly when it first emerges from the chrysalis? Show me.

THE SEASHORE

Primary Learning Objective: The children will identify and explore beach related activities while recognizing safety elements.

Materials or Equipment: None

Formation: Children are in their personal spaces.

Individual or Partner Learning Experience:
The teacher presents the following:

1. Here we are at our favorite beach. Let's begin by putting on suntan lotion. *Rub* it on your arms, legs, face, neck, and ears. This will protect you from the sun's harmful rays.

2. Show me how you can *use* your arms to make a beach umbrella. It should stand in the sun to block the sun's hot rays.

3. Who can use a hand shovel and *dig* in the sand?

4. Use your body to *make* the round shape of a beach ball. *Roll* carefully along the sand.

5. Is it possible to *walk* in the deep sand while *lifting* your legs high?

6. Let's *run* along the beach, and *jump* over a small wave.

7. Make-believe you are using a long fishing pole and *reeling* in a large fish.

8. Pretend to *blow* up a large rubber sea horse. Take a deep breath, ready, and exhale. Again, *inhale* deeply and *exhale.*

9. Time for lunch. Let's *dry* our bodies with our towels, *sit* on our blankets, *eat* lunch, *drink* water, and *rub* on more suntan lotion.

10. If you look closely, you can see small sand crabs. Crabs can walk backwards. Try to *move* like the crab by *squatting* down. Now *reach* back with both hands on the floor. Try not to let your back touch the sand. *Move* throughout the playing area like a crab.

11. Let's make the movements of the sea gull. Who can *swoop* down from the sky and *fly* low to the water?

12. It's time to play in the water. Find a buddy. Always go into the water with a buddy. Can you and your buddy *lie* at a low level on the floor and *make* a swimming motion? How many different body parts can you and your buddy use to *create* big splashes of water?

(cont.)

Whole-Group Learning Experience:
SAILING: Explain to the children that sailboats glide along the water by using the wind to push them along the water. Children are asked to make a sailboat by holding one arm straight up at the side of their heads. The other arm is stretched out to the side of the body with the palm up. This shape makes the mast of the sailboat. The imaginary sails are fastened to the masts. Challenge the children to sail throughout the playing area without touching other boats. Invite the children to find a partner and sail the two boats near each other.

THE FLEET: Inform the children that a small group of boats is called a fleet. Challenge the children to sail in a single-file line throughout the playing area with children taking turns as the lead sailboat.

A HUMAN SANDCASTLE: Inform the children that they can use their bodies to build a large human sandcastle. Ask the children who can make a tower by using their arms and pointing to the sky. See if they can make a box shape on their hands and knees. Ask the children to build their sandcastle by having some of them pretend to be blocks of sand, while others make towers with their bodies.

Creative Closure:

1. What is one activity you enjoyed participating in at the seashore?

2. Can you think of one activity we did not do today at the beach that you might enjoy doing next time? Show me.

WAVES

Primary Learning Objective: The child will gain an understanding of water movement by depicting the action of a wave individually and while working in a group.

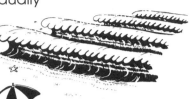

Materials or Equipment: None

Formation: Children are in their personal spaces.

Individual or Partner Learning Experience:
The teacher presents the following:

1. Today we will use our bodies to learn about waves. Waves are made from water. They begin far out at sea when the wind blows. As the waves are pushed to the land, the ocean floor stops the water from moving. The wave topples onto the land. Let's make the movement of a wave by *swinging* both of our arms back and forth. Try not to move your feet.

2. Can you make your whole body *sway* back and forth without moving your arms and feet?

3. Use your arms to make a *tumbling* action in front of your body. Your hands should *move* in circles to make this movement.

4. Show me how you can *lie* at a low level and *roll* your body like a wave coming to shore.

5. Is it possible to *roll* at a low level again and open your body into a wide shape when you stop? *Lie* very still.

Whole-Group Learning Experience:
A WAVE: Explain that the children can work together to create one large wave. The first wave is formed by asking the children to form a side-by-side line. On the count of three, the first child in line raises his or her hand, and it is grasped at a high level by the next person in line. This action is immediately followed by the next child raising his or her hand, until everyone's hand is raised.

A BIG WAVE: Ask the children to stoop in a side-by-side line. Hands remain clasped. On the count of three, the first child stands up slowly, pulling on the hand of the child beside him or her, followed by the next child rising until all of the children are standing.

A BREAKER WAVE: This wave is formed by having the children kneel in a side-by-side line. Children are no longer holding hands. The first child in line falls forward and breaks the fall by moving his or her hands forward to lower the body slowly. Encourage the children to bend their elbows as they lower their bodies. After the first child begins to fall forward, the second child begins the action, and so forth until the entire line of children has fallen forward.

Creative Closure:

1. Who can think of some places where we play in the waves (e.g., sea, ocean, lake, beach, pond, pool)?

2. Can you show me how you use your body to swim in the waves?

LIFEGUARDS

Lifeguards warn people not to swim in dangerous water,
and they rescue swimmers who need help.

1. *Rub* on your suntan lotion, *put* on your sunglasses, and hat. *Check* to see that your bottle of water is in your bag. Now it's time to *climb* to the top of the lookout chair and help all of the people at the beach to stay safe and happy.
2. *Use* make-believe binoculars to *watch* the people swimming. Find a way to *blow* a whistle, alerting the swimmers to be careful.
3. Can you *jump* down from the lookout chair while *bending* your knees and *landing* on your toes? Ready, *jump!*
4. Show me how you would *run* along the beach to make a rescue.
5. *Throw* the ring buoy to the swimmer. Now *pull* in the rope hand over hand to pull the swimmer to shore.
6. Lifeguards must be physically fit. *Jog* along the beach in the deep sand. Pretend to use heavy weights and *exercise* your arms. *Show* me the muscles in your arms.

SEA CAPTAINS

The captain is the person who navigates or steers the ship and
makes sure all the people onboard are safe, happy, and enjoying their cruise.

1. As the captain, show me how you welcome all the passengers and *shake* their hands.
2. It's time for our cruise to start. Can you *hoist* or *pull* up the sails of the ship?
3. How would you move if the ship *rocks* back and forth to the movement of the waves?
4. Can you pretend to *look* through the ship's telescope?
5. Shipmates *salute* the captain and keep the ship very clean. Make-believe you are *mopping* and *scrubbing* the ship's deck.
6. The captain *steers* the ship toward the dock as we *loosen* the sails, *roll* them up, and *tie* them down for our next voyage.

7. Now let's work together and *throw* the heavy anchor into the water.

THE SUBMARINE

Primary Learning Objective: The children will adjust their levels while moving throughout the playing area.

Materials or Equipment: None

Formation: Children are in their personal spaces.

Individual or Partner Learning Experience:
The teacher presents the following:

1. A submarine is a type of ship that can travel underwater. The word "sub" means under or below. Submarines have propellers that force the hull or body of the submarine forward. Can you *use* your arms like propellers and *move* slowly throughout the playing area?

2. See if you can change the depth of your submarine and *move* at a low level near the bottom of the ocean. Now try to *surface* at a high level.

3. A periscope is a tool that helps people see objects above the water. It is a long tube that can be raised, lowered, or moved in any direction. *Use* your arm like a periscope at a high level. *Turn* from side to side so you can see the surface of the water. *Move* the periscope down to a medium level.

Whole-Group Learning Experience:
A SUBMARINE: Divide the children into two groups. One group scatters throughout the playing area and pretends to be waves by rocking their bodies back and forth. The remainder of the children use their arms as propellers to move around the waves. Encourage the submarines to move at different levels.

GROUP SUBMARINE: Challenge the children to create one or two group submarines by using one hand to hold onto the shoulder of the person in front. The other hand acts like a propeller. The group submarine must remain in a long narrow shape as it moves throughout the waves.

Creative Closure:

1. Who can name some activities we do at a low level?

2. Show me two different ways to stretch the body at a high level.

GARDENERS

May is a good month to plant flowers and vegetable seeds in a garden. It is a gardener's responsibility to care for the lawn and the garden as flowers, fruits, and vegetables grow.

1. Who can *search* and find a spot in the yard where the sun is shining? *Point* and *move* to that spot.
2. This is a perfect spot for a garden. Show me how you *pull* the weeds from the garden.
3. Let's create a garden by using a shovel to *dig* into the earth and loosen the soil. *Pour* in some fertilizer to make the ground rich with nutrients.
4. *Dig* a small hole and *drop* in a seed. *Plant* a long row of seeds. Who can *cover* the holes with dirt and *pat* the ground? Make-believe you are a sprinkler *watering* the seeds.
5. Pretend to *snip* the hedges. *Rake* the leaves into a pile. Now let's *gather* all of those branches from the hedges and the leaves and *place* them in a large garbage bag.
6. Imagine you are *using* a lawn mower. Show me the path you would *make* when mowing around a tree, in a square, and up a hill.

LUMBERJACKS

Lumberjacks work in the deep woods.
It is their job to cut dead trees and to plant new trees.

1. Who can show me how lumberjacks *jump* out of bed and *stretch* their muscles?
2. Breakfast is very important to start each day. *Stir* a large bowl of pancake batter. Can you *flip* your pancakes as they turn golden brown? *Pour* syrup on the pancakes. Whoops! Be careful. Not too much. *Drink* your juice and your glass of milk. Let's *wash* those dishes and get ready for our day.
3. *Pull* on your heavy boots and *lace* them to the top. Who can *stomp* through the underbrush to the tall timber?
4. Let's *swing* the axe at a low level until a tree is ready to fall. Now *yell,* "tim-ber-r!" *Trim* the branches off the large tree until it looks like a log.
5. Who can pretend to *roll* the log to the truck? Now *drive* the truck to the sawmill. *Drink* a large glass of water after your hard day's work.

TIMB-ER-R!

Primary Learning Objective: The children will use their bodies to imitate the life cycle of a tree.

Materials or Equipment: None

Formation: Children are in their personal spaces.

Individual or Partner Learning Experience:
The teacher presents the following:

1. *Make* yourself into a small seedling planted deep into the ground. Show me how you begin to *grow* until you are a very large tree and can provide shade.

2. What happens as the season changes? Can you show me how the wind blows your leaves and *moves* your branches?

3. The snow is falling. Who can show how your branches freeze by making your muscles very tight?

4. The lumberjack is here and is cutting us down. Try *stretching* your arms over your head to make yourself into a very long log. Is it possible to *roll* to the river and *float* to the sawmill?

5. Can you *use* your body to show me the type of product you have become (e.g., firewood, a wooden table, wood blocks, a wooden toy train, a folded news paper)?

Whole-Group Learning Experience:
TIMB-ER-R: Designate one-third of the children to be lumberjacks. These children act as chasers and move through the forest looking for trees. The remaining children are trees and flee from the woodcutters. When a tree is tagged, the lumberjack yells, "Timb-er-r!" and the tagged tree collapses to the ground in a long, narrow log shape. After all of the trees are tagged and are lying in a log position, the lumberjacks stoop to the floor and collectively "roll" each log to the specified river area. When all the trees have been successfully rolled to the river, the children are challenged to make-believe they are planting more trees so that the activity can begin again.

Creative Closure:

1. Which body parts were used to demonstrate the actions of cutting trees?

2. What other objects have long and thin shapes? Show me.

NATURALISTS

Primary Learning Objective: The children will pretend to be animal homes and objects.

Materials or Equipment: None

Formation: Children are in their personal spaces.

Individual or Partner Learning Experience:
The teacher presents the following:

1. A naturalist is a person who knows all about outdoor life and can identify insects, animals, birds, and other living creatures. A naturalist might even discover a new type of plant or animal. Here's the backpack. Let's *pack* a camera to take photos of nature, and include a map.

2. Can you *rub* on sunscreen, *put* on a hat, and sunglasses?

3. *Hop* inside the jeep and *buckle* your seatbelt. Off we go for our adventure.

4. Our first stop is the duck pond. Can you *quack* and *waddle* like a duck? Use your body to *form* the shape of a duck's pond.

5. Insects live in the grass. *Stand* very tall and pretend to be blades of grass.

6. Squirrels find holes in tall trees to build their homes. Select a partner. With your bodies, *create* a tree and find a way to *make* a home for the squirrel.

7. Let's *skip* back to the jeep and *put* on our seatbelts. Away we go. Tomorrow is another adventure.

Whole-Group Learning Experience:
WASPS: Point to an imaginary gray nest hanging just below the tree branch. Tell the children that some wasps make their nests out of a papery substance which is dry wood moistened into a paste. Explain that they can make a paper wasp's nest by forming a large circle and having them stretch their arms either up or down. Ask three or four wasps to fly about inside the nest.

A BIRD'S NEST: Ask the children to use make-believe binoculars and look up to the bird's nest. Challenge the children to discover a way to make a round bird's nest with their bodies. One or two children can form tiny egg shapes in the middle of the nest.

LILY PADS: Explain that plants floating on top of the pond are called lily pads. Frogs jump and land on lily pads. Challenge the children to make several lily pads by having one half of the children work with partners who sit face to face. Their legs are stretched in a wide shape with partner's toes touching. The remainder of the children pretend to be frogs and jump throughout the playing area. Every frog should land on at least two lily pads.

Creative Closure:

1. Who can think of something else we might need to bring when exploring in the woods?

2. Can you name three more living creatures we might find on a walk in the woods? What do you think their homes would look like? Show me with your bodies.

THE FOREST RANGERS

Primary Learning Objective: The children will exhibit an awareness of natural objects common to the outdoor environment.

Materials or Equipment: None

Formation: Children are in their personal spaces.

Individual or Partner Learning Experience:
The teacher presents the following:

1. Forest rangers work in the forest and are responsible for protecting the land from fires. They help campers, hikers, and animals, and they teach us about life in the forest and the surrounding land. Today, Forest Ranger Marcy is driving her jeep on dirt roads and trails. We are invited to sit in her jeep and go on patrol with her. Can you *bounce* up and down as we take a ride on this bumpy dirt road?

2. Now, let's *stroll* along on an imaginary walk and *explore* the environment with Forest Ranger Marcy.

3. Hills are small piles of dirt that make the land bumpy. *Make-believe* your body is a small hill rising above the land.

4. Show me how you can *use* your arms to *form* pointed mountain peaks in a long mountain range.

5. When rain falls from the clouds quickly and then stops, this is called a rain shower. Can you *make* raindrops by *fluttering* your fingers very quickly. Now stop. Our rain shower is over.

6. Let's *jump* up and down three times while *clapping* our hands to thank Forest Ranger Marcy for sharing nature's sights with us.

Whole-Group Learning Experience:
MAKING A CAMPSITE: Ask the children to form groups of three. Challenge each group to move together to form a tent. Invite them to stretch upward on their toes while each child raises one arm to make the peak of the roof.

RAINBOWS: Remind the children that rainbows are made up of seven colors. Form a rainbow by making a side-by-side line of seven children. Ask the children to arch their arms forward to make the colors in the rainbow. The colors in the rainbow are violet, indigo (i.e., dark blue), blue, green, yellow, orange, and red.

(cont.)

RIVERS: Rivers flow in wiggly pathways across the land. Ask the children to see how many bodies they can connect by placing their hands on each other's shoulders. Challenge them to make-believe they are a long river of cold water.

A LAKE: A lake is a body of water with land surrounding it. Have some children form the lake's waves. Other children must lay very still to be the surrounding land.

ISLANDS: An island is a body of land surrounded by water. Ask the children to grasp hands to form small islands in a make-believe ocean.

Creative Closure:

1. Who can tell me their favorite color of the rainbow?

2. Can you think of another object you might find in the woods? Use your body to create this item.

CAVES

Primary Learning Objective: The child will pose his or her body in two different positions to form group cave structures.

Materials or Equipment: None

Formation: Children are in their personal spaces.

Individual or Partner Learning Experience:
The teacher presents the following:

1. Who can *use* his or her body to show me a round shape?

2. Is it possible to *enlarge* the round shape to *make* a hole?

3. Show how you can *make* a round shape with your hands and feet while *touching* the floor.

4. Select a partner and take turns *crawling* through the hole.

5. Can one partner *stand* as the second partner *crawls* between his or her legs? Use your arms and legs to *crawl* through quickly.

Whole-Group Learning Experience:
CAVES: Tell the children that a cave forms in the side of a mountain when water wears away rock and makes a hole. Divide the class into two groups. One group creates a long cave by forming a single-file line and opening their legs to make the cave. The other group crawls through the long cave structure. Exchange roles.

A TWISTING CAVE: A more complex cave is formed by having children from one group make a side-by-side line. On the teacher's signal, children bend forward so that their weight is supported by their hands and feet. The remaining children crawl under this long cave structure. Exchange roles.

Creative Closure:

1. Who can name some animals and creatures that live in caves (e.g., bears, bats, salamanders, spiders, snakes)?

2. Show me how these animals and creatures move.

RIVER ROCKS

Primary Learning Objective: The children will improve their balance skills while also demonstrating an understanding of spatial awareness.

Materials or Equipment: Nonslip carpet mats or rugs, chalk, tape, and lively music

Formation: Children are in their personal spaces.

Individual or Partner Learning Experience:
The teacher presents the following:

1. Can you *balance* on one foot while *stretching* your arms out to the sides? Try to *balance* while placing your hands and arms elsewhere. Show me how you can *balance* while *standing* on your other foot. Who can *balance* while *bending* your knee? Find a way to *balance* with three body parts *touching* the floor.

2. With a partner, have one person *balance* on one leg while the other person offers a helping hand to maintain the balance. Can you *use* another upper body part to help your partner maintain a good balance? Exchange roles.

Whole-Group Learning Experience:
RIVER ROCKS: Explain to the children that algae is an organism that lives in water or wet soil. Some algae is so small that we need a microscope to see it. Algae helps purify our air and water. Blue-green algae can coat rocks and make them slippery or slimy. Scatter river rocks (different sizes and shapes if possible) throughout the playing area. The children are told that in order to feel cool they can swim in the river. But, they must be careful because there is algae drifting in the river. As music plays, it is safe to "swim around" the river rocks.

When the music stops, all children must move to a rock so that no part of their bodies are touching the water. The river rocks are varied in size to hold one or more children. If any part of the body, including shoes, is in the "river," the floating blue-green algae will cover them. Instead of the children being eliminated, the teacher uses an imaginary hose to wash off algae. As the activity continues, rocks can be removed one at a time, or made smaller for a greater challenge.

'RITHMETIC RIVER ROCKS: Give the children a simple math problem (e.g., 2 + 1 = 3, 5 − 3 = 2). The children respond by placing that number of bodies on a river rock. If there are not enough children to create enough groups to equal the answer, hands and other body parts may be raised into the air to be counted.

Creative Closure:

1. What body parts did you use to balance on the rock?

2. Show me how you can run, stop, and balance on one foot quickly.

JUNGLE VINES

Primary Learning Objective: The children will improve their agility and cooperation while participating in jungle-themed fitness activities.

Materials or Equipment: Chalk or tape, one jump rope five to six feet in length, and one 10- to 16-foot jump rope

Formation: Children are scattered throughout the playing area.

Individual or Partner Learning Experience:
The teacher presents the following:

1. Can you *jump* high in the air to *catch* an imaginary jungle vine?

2. Show me how you can *jump* forward for distance. Try to *swing* your arms forward and *land* on bent knees as if swinging on a vine.

3. Is it possible to *jump* over a swamp (i.e., two parallel lines approximately two feet wide) without getting your sneakers "wet?" The teacher can vary the width of the swamp depending on the physical abilities of the children.

Whole-Group Learning Experience:
JUMP THE VINE: Explain to the children they will increase their fitness by playing a series of jump rope activities in which the jump rope remains close to the floor. Assign two children to be turners. The turners hold the rope stationary on the floor. All other children form a line facing the rope several feet away and take turns jumping over the rope without touching it. The first child then goes around the turner and joins the back of the line. When the first child gets to the front of the line again, the rope is raised a few inches higher. Older children can have the height of the rope adjusted higher for an additional challenge. Exchange roles.

SUPER SNAKE: The turners are on their knees and shake the rope back and forth across the floor. The children try to jump over the snake (i.e., rope) without touching it. There is a continual flow of children who return to the back of the line after jumping.

JUNGLE RIVER IS RISING: The turners are on their knees and shake the rope up and down to create small waves. Start with low waves and then gradually increase the intensity. The jumpers try to jump over the waves.

HERE COMES THE VINE: The turners swing the rope from side to side. A jumper can start in the middle and jump as the rope approaches his or her body. The children who successfully jump over the "vine" can increase their number of jumps (e.g., first attempt, each child tries one time; second turn, each child tries to jump twice, etc.)

RUN THROUGH THE JUNGLE: The turners continuously turn the rope clockwise a full rotation, and the jumper runs under the rope without touching it.

Creative Closure:

1. What parts of your body did you use to help you jump higher over the rope?

2. Does anyone have a favorite jump rope game that we could play? Show us.

SCIENTISTS

Scientists explore and discover facts about the world we live in.

1. Show me how you can *mix* the chemicals found in medicines.
2. *Curl* your hands. *Place* one hand on top of the other to create a make-believe microscope. *Look* through the microscope and *move* like the imaginary objects you see.
3. Scientists study weather conditions. Pretend to be the rain *sprinkling* downward, clouds *floating*, wind *swirling*, and lightning *shooting* through the sky.
4. Scientists study the planets and stars. Who can be the sun *rising* and *setting*? Can you be the earth *spinning* around the sun?
5. Scientists study how plants and animals grow. Is it possible to be small like an acorn and slowly *grow* into a tall tree? Pretend to *hatch* from an egg and then *walk* and *strut* like a rooster.

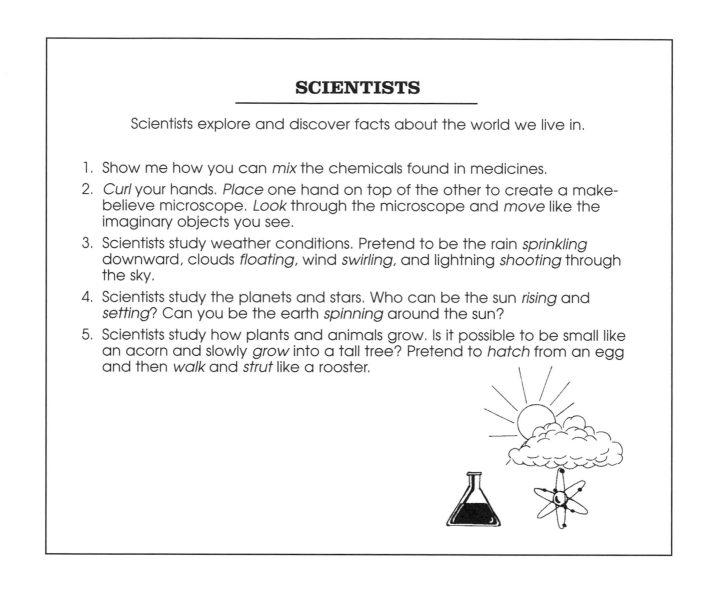

WEATHER FORECASTERS

Primary Learning Objective: The children will comprehend changing wind patterns by performing a variety of moderate to vigorous movements associated with the Beaufort Scale.

Materials or Equipment: None

Formation: Children are in their personal spaces.

Individual or Partner Learning Experience:
The teacher presents the following:

1. The weather forecaster shares weather information with people. The weather forecaster also warns people if a large storm is approaching. The greatest cause of weather is wind. Large masses of air, some of which are hot and some cool, are constantly moving over the earth's surface. The Beaufort (bō´fərt) Scale is used to classify wind strength. Use your body to move like the following actions associated with the Beaufort Scale.

   Rating: 0
   Effects on Land: Calm, smoke rises straight upward.
   Movement Experience: Can you slowly *raise* your bodies upward?

   Rating: 1
   Effects on Land: Weather vanes are inactive. Smoke drifts gently.
   Movement Experience: *Move* smoothly throughout the playing area.

   Rating: 2
   Effects on Land: Wind is felt on the face. Leaves rustle.
   Movement Experience: See if you can *run* and *feel* the wind on your face.

   Rating: 3
   Effects on Land: Leaves and twigs start to move. Light flags begin to unfurl.
   Movement Experience: Make a *fluttering* motion with your fingers and arms.

   Rating: 4
   Effects on Land: Small branches sway. Dust and papers are blowing around.
   Movement Experience: Try to *hold* your hands close and in front of your body. Make a *swishing* motion back and forth.

   Rating: 5
   Effects on Land: Small trees sway. Whitecaps are visible on water waves.
   Movement Experience: Find a way to *sway* your upper body back and forth smoothly.

   Rating: 6
   Effects on Land: Large branches move.
   Movement Experience: Show me how you can *shake* your arms and legs vigorously.

   Rating: 7
   Effects on Land: Whole trees move. Walking is difficult.
   Movement Experience: Pretend to *walk* by *leaning* forward in heavy wind.

(cont.)

Rating: 8
Effects on Land: Twigs break off.
Movement Experience: Make a *bending* motion in your arms.

Rating: 9
Effects on Land: Chimneys blow off roofs.
Movement Experience: *Jump* into the air and pretend to *crash* to the ground.

Rating: 10
Effects on Land: Trees are uprooted.
Movement Experience: *Fall* forward from a standing position. *Use* hands to cushion your fall.

Rating: 11-17
Effects on Land: Widespread damage and destruction.
Movement Experience: Pretend to be in a tropical storm, *moving* vigorously throughout the playing area.

2. With a partner, can you *hold* hands while a very strong wind is blowing in your face and trying to push you backward?

3. While still holding hands with your partner, show me how you would *move* if the strong wind is hitting your back and *pushing* your forward.

Whole-Group Learning Experience:
IMAGINARY THUNDERSTORM: Challenge the children to create all of the movements common to a thunderstorm (e.g., wind, hail, cloud movement, lightning, crashing thunder, rain).

Creative Closure:

1. Animals and sea creatures can sense changes in approaching weather conditions. When strong winds, with a rating of 7, are approaching, who can demonstrate what birds might do? (Birds fly away.)

2. If we have winds rated 12, this would be a hurricane. Can you spin your bodies like the winds of a hurricane?

Assessing Movement-Based Learning

ASSESSING AGE AND STAGE APPROPRIATE CONTENT

There are numerous textbooks available to teachers and teacher trainers that identify a variety of strategies used to assess behaviors of three- to eight-year-old children (Beaty, 1992; Bredekamp & Copple, 2004; Leong & McAfee, 1994; Van Hoorn, Nourot, Scales, & Alward, 2003; Warner & Sower, 2005). The majority of these resources discuss the advantages and disadvantages of each strategy and use examples of generally accepted content (e.g., the child's ability to identify colors or body parts by an expected age) to show how the user can judge the extent to which learning has occurred. In each resource, the focus is on determining if the child reaches the identified goal.

This chapter contains four sample assessment rubrics to assist the teacher in ascertaining the extent to which a child participates within an individual, partner, and whole-group learning experience. It also includes a teacher self-assessment form and ways to motivate children to assess their involvement and enjoyment of the activity.

Involving the Child in the Assessment Process

Preschool and elementary age children can be very creative when motivated to give their thoughts about the lesson (i.e., what they liked, didn't like, and what they would do to improve the movement experience). In the simplest sense, the teacher can use the creative closure as a form of child assessment. The teacher can also ask the children to rate the lesson by raising their hands (e.g., raise your hand if you think it was excellent, or good, or poor), or the teacher might ask the children to rate the lesson by showing the appropriate number of fingers (e.g., three as excellent, two as good, and one as poor). In addition, the children can be asked to rate the lesson by displaying a smile, pout, frown, or no expression. The following identifies additional ways to determine the child's assessment of the lesson:

1. Displaying thumbs up, thumbs to the side, or thumbs down.
2. Asking the children to stand tall if they liked the lesson, to place their hands on their knees if the lesson was "OK," or to sit if they did not enjoy the lesson.
3. Jumping forward, standing in place, or jumping back.
4. Taking a giant step forward, standing in place, or taking a giant step back.
5. Standing with hands on hips while bending forward and upward shows "yes," hands on hips twisting side to side symbolizes "OK," or saying "no" by stretching to touch the floor.
6. Asking the children to stand in front of a green colored paper taped to the wall signifying "yes," a yellow paper representing "good," or a red paper meaning "poor."
7. Writing a check-plus (✓+), which is good, or a check-minus (✓−), which is poor, on a piece of paper
8. Drawing a favorite activity within the lesson or drawing an aspect of the lesson that they did not enjoy as much.
9. Asking the children to draw or write something they learned, something they thought was important to know, or something they recalled from the movement-based lesson.

SAMPLE ASSESSMENT

Assessing the Child's Participation within an *Individual* Learning Experience

	4	3	2	1
Teacher's Name: _____	ALWAYS	USUALLY	SOMETIMES	NEVER
Child's Name: _____				
Age/Grade: _____				
Learning Experience: _____				
Date: _____				

TOTAL SCORE

CIRCLE THE APPROPRIATE NUMBER FOR EACH CRITERIA

Within the Cognitive/Intellectual Domain:				
The child identifies the name of the body parts.	4	3	2	1
The child visualizes items that cannot be seen.	4	3	2	1
The child imagines the body is manipulating an object.	4	3	2	1
Within the Affective/Social Domain:				
The child uses the body to express feelings and emotions.	4	3	2	1
The child feels and shows confidence in trying novel ways of moving.	4	3	2	1
The child appreciates the roles and actions of people or things that influence one's life.	4	3	2	1
Within the Psychomotor/Physical Domain:				
The child imitates or duplicates the common movements of objects or things.	4	3	2	1
The child uses combinations of body parts to produce one whole movement.	4	3	2	1
The child successfully demonstrates movement skills within moderate to vigorous physical activity.	4	3	2	1
The child responds physically to creative closure question.	4	3	2	1

Additional Comments: _____

_____

_____

Assessing the Child's Participation within a *Partner* Learning Experience

Teacher's Name: _____

Child's Name: _____

Age/Grade: _____

Learning Experience: _____

Date: _____

TOTAL SCORE

	4	3	2	1
	EXCELLENT INTERACTION	GOOD INTERACTION	SOMEWHAT INTERACTIVE	NO INTERACTION
	Always	Usually	Sometimes	

CIRCLE THE APPROPRIATE NUMBER FOR EACH CRITERIA

Within the Cognitive/Intellectual Domain:				
The child recalls past experiences to yield new movement patterns with a partner.	4	3	2	1
The child discovers how to link movements together with a partner.	4	3	2	1
The child discusses facts related to objects or things with a partner.	4	3	2	1
Within the Affective/Social Domain:				
The child assists a partner in the demonstration of the activity.	4	3	2	1
The child is willing to switch roles with a partner.	4	3	2	1
The child shows respect for a partner's strengths, weaknesses, or disability.	4	3	2	1
Within the Psychomotor/Physical Domain:				
The child stretches a group of body parts with a partner.	4	3	2	1
The child manipulates a partner's body to move in a specific way.	4	3	2	1
The child explores multiple movement responses with a partner.	4	3	2	1

Additional Comments: _____

_____

_____

SAMPLE ASSESSMENT	**Assessing the Child's Participation within a *Whole-Group* Learning Experience**				

	4	**3**	**2**	**1**
Teacher's Name: _____	ALWAYS	USUALLY	SOMETIMES	NEVER
Child's Name: _____				
Age/Grade: _____	**TOTAL SCORE**			
Learning Experience: _____				
Date: _____	CIRCLE THE APPROPRIATE NUMBER FOR EACH CRITERIA			

Within the Cognitive/Intellectual Domain:				
The child differentiates between what is "fantasy" and "real" within a whole-group activity.	4	3	2	1
The child responds verbally to suggestions made by group members.	4	3	2	1
The child critiques success level and shows enthusiasm for whole-group tasks.	4	3	2	1
Within the Affective/Social Domain:				
The child shares ideas freely with others.	4	3	2	1
The child demonstrates cooperative gestures with others.	4	3	2	1
The child contributes suggestions for completing group activities.	4	3	2	1
Within the Psychomotor/Physical Domain:				
The child participates physically in all group activities.	4	3	2	1
The child finds ways to improve upon the group movement response.	4	3	2	1
The child responds successfully to whole-group challenges involving small or large muscle control.	4	3	2	1

Additional Comments: _____
_____
_____

SAMPLE ASSESSMENT

Teacher's Self-Assessment

Teacher's Name: ______________________

Date: __________ Setting: ______________

Number of Children: __________ Age/Grade: __________

Learning Experience: ______________________

RATING SCALE
High 5 – 1 Low

Circle the appropriate number for each criteria

	REFLECTION	RATING
Did the children comprehend the purpose of the learning experience?		5 4 3 2 1
Were there movement or classroom concepts in the learning experience that were unknown to the children?		5 4 3 2 1
Were there challenges in the learning experience that frustrated the children?		5 4 3 2 1
Did I ask the children to think of different ways to solve problems and propose alternative solutions?		5 4 3 2 1
Did the children express themselves freely and joyously?		5 4 3 2 1
Did children interact and cooperate with classmates in the learning experience?		5 4 3 2 1
Were there class conflicts that did not resolve quickly and in a positive manner?		5 4 3 2 1
Did I encourage cooperation and praise group efforts?		5 4 3 2 1
Did my voice and enthusiasm stimulate the child's imagination?		5 4 3 2 1
Was I sensitive to all attempts at creativity, no matter how simple?		5 4 3 2 1
Did I offer encouragement to children who were reluctant to express themselves?		5 4 3 2 1
Did I establish a safe environment for active participation?		5 4 3 2 1
Were there moderate physical movements that children did not successfully perform after additional assistance?		5 4 3 2 1
Were there vigorous movements that children did not successfully perform after additional assistance?		5 4 3 2 1

Additional Teacher's Reflections: ______________________

____

____

Acknowledgements

The authors would like to extend their sincere appreciation to the school administrators, faculty, staff, and, of course, the children of the following schools or learning centers whose expertise greatly strengthened the contents of this book.

Calvary Lutheran Nursery School, East Meadow, New York

Central Islip Union Free School District Early Childhood Center, Central Islip, New York

Jewish Community Center of West Hempstead Nursery School, West Hempstead, New York

Levittown Union Free School District, Levittown, New York

Messa Education Centre, Mwanza, Tanzania, East Africa

Mineola Union Free School District, Mineola, New York

MSAD #22, Hampden, Maine

Progressive School of Long Island, Merrick, New York

Saltzman Community Services Center, Hempstead, New York

A special thanks to the students who are majoring in Early Childhood and Elementary Education from Hofstra University's Department of Curriculum and Teaching and graduate students from Manhattanville College majoring in Physical Education and Sport Pedagogy, who have also shared their thoughts and ideas regarding the book's content. We gratefully acknowledge the creative talents of Roseann Carboy, Michelle Merriweather, Judith Taylor, Sari Goldberg, Rondi Salomon, Nicole De Felice, Stephanie Kaltsas, and Lauren Casal.

We would like to acknowledge the following people who provided their expertise: Karen O'Sullivan, Graphic Designer, G.H.C. Illustrations; John C. Farrell, Publications Manager, National Association for Sport and Physical Education; Mike Lee and Joyce Zucker, Child's Play Specialists; Eileen Collins, Curriculum Specialist and Principal; Arlene Jurofsky, Environmental Specialist; Gabi and Sully Diamond, Culture Specialists; Paula Steinberg, Special Education and Autism Specialist; Doris and Harold Steinberg and Leonard Feingersch, Child Specialists; Rose Schneider, Literacy Specialist; and at the Progressive School of Long Island, Eric Jacobson, Elementary School Founder and Director; Jennifer LaRossa and Deborah Denson, Grade One Teachers; and Beth Obergh, Art Teacher.

We would also like to recognize Doris P. Fromberg, Ed. D., Department Chairperson, and Shelley B. Wepner, Ed. D., Dean for their administrative support in this project.

Finally, we would like to express our love and gratitude to Sylvia J. Giallombardo, Jay Schneider, Marcy Schneider, Scott Schneider, our family members, who have been there every step of the way in our endeavors to write this book.

About The Authors

Rhonda L. Clements, Ed.D.

Rhonda L. Clements, Ed.D., is a Professor of Education within the Department of Educational Leadership and Special Subjects at Manhattanville College in Purchase, New York, where she is the Program Director of the MAT in Physical Education and Sport Pedagogy. She received her Doctorate of Education at Teachers College, Columbia University from the Department of Movement Sciences and Education, where she studied early childhood developmental characteristics and movement activities for children. Since that time, she has authored or edited nine books in the area of movement, play, and game activities for children. She has also written more than 20 articles concerning the need for play for preschool and elementary school age children, including seven book chapters. She has presented at more than 40 international or national conferences and at over 60 state and local conferences. Dr. Clements was one of eight national experts to contribute to the document entitled, *Active Start: A Statement of Physical Activity Guidelines for Birth to Five Years,* which was sponsored by the National Association for Sport and Physical Education. She was also the recipient of the *Early Childhood News* Director Award in the curriculum category for the Let's Move, Let's Play Product.

In addition, Dr. Clements is the past president of The American Association For the Child's Right to Play (IPA/USA), a United Nations recognized association composed of experts in child development, play theories, and play practices in 44 countries, whose primary purpose is to protect, preserve, and promote play throughout the world. Dr. Clements has also served as a consultant to numerous state education departments, the US Department of Health and Human Services to train Native American Head Start Specialists, Delmar Publishing, Small World Press, Nabisco, NAEYC, SECA, Kindercare, Children's Television Network/Sesame Street, Nick Jr., Family Magazine, The Disney Channel, Crayola Crayons, and Parental Wisdom. She conducted a national survey for Wisk Laundry Detergent aimed at investigating the extent to which children are playing outdoors today compared to the previous generation.

Dr. Clements has appeared on more that 90 radio and television stations throughout the country, and has been interviewed by more than 250 journalists and newspaper reporters on the subject of child's play. Her research interests focus on historical and contemporary sociocultural issues in play, play provisions, physical activity, as well as sports throughout the world. She is currently the Associate Editor of the on-line journal, *PlayRights: An International Journal of the Theory and Practice of Play.*

Sharon L. Schneider, MS.

Sharon Schneider is an adjunct assistant professor and movement specialist within the Department of Curriculum and Teaching at Hofstra University, Hempstead, New York.

Sharon teaches a number of required early childhood and elementary education courses on the undergraduate and graduate levels relating to child movement, music, and play within the curriculum for the classroom teacher. She is also the physical educator at the Progressive School of Long Island in Merrick, New York, a private school for children in kindergarten through grade seven. Ms. Schneider has also taught in the classroom and within inclusion settings.

Ms. Schneider received her Master of Science degree in Physical Education from Hofstra University, New York; studied Recreational Administration at Brooklyn College, New York; and received her Bachelor of Science degree in Physical Education and Health from Long Island University, Brooklyn, New York. As a member of the American Association for the Child's Right to Play (IPA/USA), Sharon serves on the board as the National Chairperson for Afterschool Play Issues.

In the areas of physical education, recreation, and play, Sharon has enjoyed implementing programs for the preschool through geriatric age population and is recognized as a leader in the field of purposeful play, fun-filled, and creative activities. She has worked in New York, New Jersey, as well as her local Long Island community for schools, afterschool programs, community centers, summer camp programs, organizations including PTA, SEPTA, Cub Scouts, Girl Scouts, as a physical educator, classroom teacher, recreational leader, coach, volunteer, and consultant.

Having presented at international, national, and state conferences, Sharon's topics have focused on child movement, creative play, themed activities, integrating academic concepts utilizing movement and props, community playdays, physical activity, and health. She has written numerous articles, and has most recently contributed to Gryphon House Publishing.

Sharon helps parents of children with special needs. She also provides staff development and is a consultant for recess curriculums, afterschool programs, preschools, and elementary schools. She and her husband Jay reside in Franklin Square, New York, with their children Marcy and Scott.

Learning Experiences Index

Living Creatures and the Environment Learning Experiences

Assessing Movement-Based Learning

References

Bandura, A. (1977). *Social learning theory.* Englewood Cliffs, NJ: Prentise Hall.

Beaty, J. J. (1992). *Observing development of the young child* (3rd ed.). New York: Merrill/Macmillan.

Bredekamp, S., & Copple, C. (2004). *Developmentally appropriate practice in early childhood programs* (Revised ed.). Washington, DC: National Association for the Education of Young Children.

Erickson, E. (1963). *Childhood and society* (2nd ed.) New York: Norton.

Froebel, F. W. A. (1887). *The education of man.* (W. N. Hailmann, Trans.). New York: Appleton. (Original work published 1826)

Graham, G., Holt/Hale, S., & Parker, M. (2004). *Children moving: A reflective approach to teaching physical education with PowerWeb.* New York: McGraw-Hill.

Leong, D., & McAfee, O. (1994). *Assessing and guiding: Young children's development and learning.* Boston: Allyn & Bacon.

National Association for Sport and Physical Education. (2002). *Active start: A statement of physical activity guidelines for children birth to five years.* Reston, VA: Author.

National Association for Sport and Physical Education. (2004a). *Moving into the future: National standards for physical education* (2nd ed.). Reston, VA: Author.

National Association for Sport and Physical Education. (2004b). *Physical activity for children: A statement of guidelines for children ages 5-12.* Reston, VA: Author.

Piaget, J. (1962). *Play, dreams, and imitation in childhood.* New York: Norton.

Roberts, J. (2001). *The origins of fruits and vegetables.* New York: Universe.

Singer, J. L. (1973). *The child's world of make-believe: Experimental studies of imaginative play.* New York: Academic Press.

Skinner, B. F. (1974) *About behaviorism.* New York: Knopf.

Van Hoorn, J., Nourot, P. M., Scales, B., & Alward, K. R. (2003). *Play at the center of the curriculum* (3rd ed.). Upper Saddle River, NJ: Prentice Hall.

Warner, L., & Sower, J. (2005). *Educating young children from preschool through primary grades.* Boston: Allyn & Bacon.

Resources

Published by the National Association for Sport and Physical Education for quality physical education programs:

Moving into the Future: National Standards for Physical Education, 2nd edition (2004), Stock No. 304-10275

Physical Educators' Guide to Successful Grant Writing (2005), Stock No. 304-10291

Physical Activity for Children: A Statement of Guidelines (2004), Stock No. 304-10276

On Your Mark... Get Set... Go!: A Guide for Beginning Physical Education Teachers (2004), Stock No. 304-10264

Ask-PE: Physical Education Concepts Test CD-ROM (2004), Stock No. 304-10271P & 304-10271M

Concepts and Principles of Physical Education: What Every Student Needs to Know (2003), Stock No. 304-10261

Beyond Activities: Elementary Volume (2003), Stock No. 304-10265

Beyond Activities: Secondary Volume (2003), Stock No. 304-10268

National Physical Education Standards in Action (2003), Stock No. 304-10267

National Standards for Beginning Physical Education Teachers (2003), Stock No. 304-10273

Active Start: A Statement of Physical Activity Guidelines for Children Birth to Five Years (2002), Stock No. 304-10254

Appropriate Practice Documents

Appropriate Practice in Movement Programs for Young Children, (2000), Stock No. 304-10232

Appropriate Practices for Elementary School Physical Education (2000), Stock No. 304-10230

Appropriate Practices for Middle School Physical Education (2001), Stock No. 304-10248

Appropriate Practices for High School Physical Education (2004), Stock No. 304-10272

Opportunity to Learn Documents

Opportunity to Learn Standards for Elementary Physical Education (2000), Stock No. 304-10242

Opportunity to Learn Standards for Middle School Physical Education (2004), Stock No. 304-10290

Opportunity to Learn Standards for High School Physical Education (2004), Stock No. 304-10289

Assessment Series

Assessment of Swimming in Physical Education (2005), Stock No. 304-10301

Assessing Dance in Elementary Physical Education (2005), Stock No. 304-10304

Assessing Concepts: Secondary Biomechanics (2004), Stock No. 304-10220

Assessment in Outdoor Adventure Physical Education (2003), Stock No. 304-10218

Assessing Student Outcomes in Sport Education (2003), Stock No. 304-10219

Video Tools for Teaching Motor Skill Assessment (2002), Stock No. 304-10217

Assessing Heart Rate in Physical Education (2002), Stock No. 304-10214

Authentic Assessment of Physical Activity for High School Students (2002), Stock No. 304-10216

Portfolio Assessment for K-12 Physical Education (2000), Stock No. 304-10213

Elementary Heart Health: Lessons and Assessment (2001), Stock No. 304-10215

Standards-Based Assessment of Student Learning: A Comprehensive Approach (1999), Stock No. 304-10206

Assessment in Games Teaching (1999), Stock No. 304-10212

Assessing Motor Skills in Elementary Physical Education (1999), Stock No. 304-10207

Assessing and Improving Fitness in Elementary Physical Education (1999), Stock No. 304-10208

Creating Rubrics for Physical Education (1999), Stock No. 304-10209

Assessing Student Responsibility and Teamwork (1999), Stock No. 304-10210

Preservice Professional Portfolio System (1999), Stock No. 304-10211

Order online at www.naspeinfo.org or call 1-800-321-0789
Shipping and handling additional

National Association for Sport and Physical Education
an association of the American Alliance for Health, Physical Education, Recreation, and Dance
1900 Association Drive, Reston, VA 20191, naspe@aahperd.org, 703-476-3410